Pioneer-at-Law

Foreword by Earl Warren

CHIEF JUSTICE OF THE UNITED STATES, RETIRED

Pioneer-at-Law

Geo. Clifton Edwards

"THE PIONEER"

by *GEORGE EDWARDS*

New York W · W · NORTON & COMPANY · INC ·

CREDIT: The photograph on the title page is by the *Dallas Morning News*, 1954.

FIRST EDITION

Library of Congress Cataloging in Publication Data
Edwards, George Clifton, Jr. 1914–
    Pioneer-at-law.
    1. Edwards, George Clifton, d. 1961. I. Title.
KF373.E28E3   340'.092'4 [B]   74-7372
ISBN 0-393-07483-8

1 2 3 4 5 6 7 8 9 0

*To my beloved wife Peg, who lived the
writing of every page of this book with me.*

CONTENTS

FOREWORD

THIS IS THE LIFE story of a man without ambition for fortune or fame in a strictured society but who, with compassion and dignity, dedicated a long professional career with profound lasting effects to the cause of the poor, the under-privileged, and the oppressed. He, of course, was never accorded either fame or fortune, and without flinching he willingly accepted a share of the obliq-uity inflicted upon his clients and the causes he pursued as a lawyer in the courts of his state.

The story is told by an adoring son who, through honoring the heritage thus left to him and by pur-suing similar causes with like dedication as a judge on some of the higher courts of the nation, has achieved much of the distinction his father earned but was never accorded.

Throughout the book is evidence of the effect of wholesome family life where both father and mother devoted their lives and their parental influ-ences to the causes of education and justice. It car-ries with it the assurance that under our system of government even one person whose efforts may be unsung can play an important part in changing for the better the mores not only of his community, but also of his state and the nation.

It should fascinate and strengthen the resolve of all who cherish a satisfying life based on conscience and a sense of justice for all people in keeping with our pledge of "one nation under God, indivisible, with liberty and justice for all."

The book should also inspire and comfort those who might doubt the worthwhileness and efficacy, in our complex society, of individual effort in the face of adversity. In short, it is a wholesome and meaningful American success story for all of us in these troublesome times through which we are now passing.

EARL WARREN

Chief Justice of the United States, Retired

ACKNOWLEDGMENTS

THE WRITING of a book is an adventure in itself. Those whose names are listed below were involved with me in this adventure in some very meaningful way. Each gave valuable help either in research or in editorial comment after reading some or all of the manuscript. Some of the contributions were so important that without them *Pioneer-at-Law* would never have been published. To each of those listed below I express great appreciation; but I am the only one responsible for the contents of this book.

Carl Brannin, Frank Harrison, Sarah Hughes, George Lambert, James P. Simpson, A. Maceo Smith, Nat Wells, all of Dallas, Texas; Frank Winn of Dallas, Detroit, and (now) Woodstock, Vermont.

John Dorsey, Martin Hayden, Damon Keith, Golda Krolik, Ken Morris, Theodore Souris, all of Detroit, Michigan; Kathy and James Edwards of Lansing, Michigan.

Margaret Edwards, Agnes W. Ingles, Mimi Levinson, Regine Ransohoff, all of Cincinnati, Ohio.

Virginia and Harry Phillips of Nashville, Tennessee.

Joseph P. Lash, Harry Steeger, both of New York City.

Mary and John Herling of Washington, D.C.

Sharon and George C. Edwards of Detroit, Michigan, and Washington, D.C.

Special acknowledgment is due to three librarians without whose help the research essential to this book could not have been accomplished: Phil Mason and Warner Pflug, Archives of Labor History and Urban Affairs, Wayne State University, Detroit, Michigan; Lucile A. Boykin, Texas History and Genealogy Division, Dallas Public Library, Dallas, Texas.

Special thanks are also due to my sister, Octavia Nichols Edwards, of Dallas and New York City, for supplying many of the intimate recollections that are included in this volume and for valuable editorial assistance.

Finally, I owe a profound debt for whatever virtues this book may have to my editor at W. W. Norton & Company, Evan Thomas. After accepting the first draft of this book, he furnished such a list of editorial suggestions that it took me a full year and a half to work through them. In the end, thanks to him, it is a very different book and, I believe, a very much better one.

Pioneer-at-Law

THE SENATE HEARING

THE HEARING ROOM was paneled in oak and impressive, as befits the Judiciary Committee of the United States Senate. The five senators—Ervin, Dirksen, Hruska, Olin Johnson, and Hart—sat on a raised dais built in a semicircle facing the witness.

The southern accent of the witness took me back nostalgically to my Texas boyhood, until I heard him say, "A leopard does not change its spots." I was the leopard under discussion. The speaker was the president of the Chattanooga Bar Association. He and other Tennessee Bar Association leaders had been talking about my youth and about my father. Much of what they had said was true, although it did not seem to me to add up to his conclusion that the United States Senate should refuse to advise and consent to President Kennedy's nomination of me as a United States circuit judge.

My appointment had been proposed by Pat McNamara, Michigan's senior senator, who sat beside me now. Historically, the judgeship was conceived to be Michigan's concern, since I was to replace a Michigan judge. I had passed the alphabetical tests of the ABA and the FBI and I had solid—indeed, practically unanimous—support from my state. In

twenty-four years of public life—mostly elective—
the voters of Michigan had been generous to me. I
was just completing an active term as police com-
missioner of Detroit.

Nonetheless, I had not viewed the Senate hearings with equanimity. In 1958 FBI director J. Edgar
Hoover had delivered a speech at the American Bar
Association Convention in Los Angeles attacking
the juvenile courts. The Council of Judges of the
National Council on Crime and Delinquency, of
which I was a member, defended them. I had
helped draft the resolution. We had suggested that
Hoover stick to investigating and leave judging to
the judges. Hoover had sent FBI agents to see
nearly every judge on the council to demand a re-
traction—a demand that had not been met.

Repercussions of our temerity were still vibrat-
ing when McNamara proposed to nominate me as a
circuit judge.

McNamara was a strong senator, popular with
his fellow senators, and also known to them as a bad
man to have as an enemy. Michigan's other senator,
Phil Hart, was a close friend of mine and a member
of the Senate Judiciary Committee. The then attorney general, Robert Kennedy, and I shared a joint
interest in the fight against organized crime. I was
accustomed to defending my public record of
twenty-four years—most of it in the Michigan
courts. But I knew the twenty-four years from birth
to the first public office contained a lot of colorful
material for critics to work on.

I also knew that the Los Angeles resolution had not been forgotten and that any FBI investigation would be considerably more than casual. It was. In the end, however, the record made in public office prevailed, and on Labor Day in 1963 from Hyannis Port President Kennedy sent my nomination to the Senate.

I don't know just who conveyed to the Tennessee Bar Association the complete dossier on my father, on my youth in Dallas, and on my earliest years in Detroit, but somebody certainly did. The Tennessee Bar Association erupted and had continued to erupt up to this, the second hearing day.

Senator Ervin had just asked the Chattanooga bar president whether he had read any of the 248 opinions I had written as a member of the Michigan Supreme Court. He had answered no, but had gone on to insist on the immutability of the influences of my youth—particularly that of my father. As I listened, I knew that very shortly I would be called back to the table where the Chattanooga bar president now sat.

The advice and consent of the United States Senate to appointment of a federal appellate judge is a political judgment of high order. It is the business of the Senate to search out any arguably relevant factors, positive or negative, which could be cited about any nominee for a judgeship. While my opponents from the Tennessee bar hardly delighted me at the time, I had no doubt about their sincerity or their right to express their opposition.

Senator Ervin, now of Watergate fame, chaired both hearings. He is a respected constitutional lawyer and a former justice of the Supreme Court of North Carolina. He handled the two hearings with thoroughness, patience, courtesy, and an occasional bit of humor. He had taken the trouble to read a good sample of my Michigan Supreme Court opinions. At the first hearing he had seen that the record, pro and con, was very complete. I could not ask for fairer treatment.

Also, to what point would one debate the issues that moved my father in 1906 to run for governor of Texas on the Socialist ticket, or that moved me in 1933 to circulate the Oxford Pledge against war on the campus of Southern Methodist University? The issue before the committee was what sort of judge I had been and could be expected to be in 1963 and beyond.

I decided not to dispute the leopard analogy. But I also decided some day to write about the spots on the leopard.

This hearing took place on November 21, 1963. The next day President John F. Kennedy was killed in Dallas. Such emotions as the hearing had produced were replaced by much deeper ones. President Johnson's renomination of me and the Senate's confirmation were profoundly overshadowed by the national tragedy.

I doubt that any subject of a disputed Senate confirmation hearing will ever completely forget the experience, but no ill-will lingers from mine. What remained with me in the aftermath was a doubt that I had done justice to someone who hadn't been there at all. Dad wasn't the nominee; I hadn't thought it relevant—or possible in terms of time—to explain his life or adequately to defend him. At one point Senator Johnson (of South Carolina), with evident friendly intent toward me, observed that a man should not be blamed for the sins of his father. He commented that he had known sons of drunken fathers who didn't touch a drop. As will be obvious, the analogies did not seem apt to me.

What follows does not purport to discuss (let alone account for) all of the spots on this leopard. A good deal of the concern of the Senate hearing was focused on events in the early days of the labor movement in Detroit. But the auto plants of Detroit are 1,200 miles from Main Street in Dallas, and a world apart. To me they are basically very different stories.

This is, in part, the story of a somewhat different boyhood in Texas in the decades of the twenties and thirties. Principally, however, it is the story of my father's life. It is what I would like to have had time to tell the senators about attorney Geo. Clifton Edwards of Dallas, Texas—a very different kind of American pioneer.

THE MINISTRY OF
THE COTTON MILL

BY STRANGE coincidence my father's life story really began very close to Chattanooga, Tennessee. Twenty miles northwest of there, as the crow flies, lies the University of the South, situated on top of one of the most beautiful of the Cumberland Mountains. Dad registered for college at Sewanee (as this college is better known) in 1894. He was born and brought up in Dallas, Texas, but as was true of many Texans, he had deep roots in Tennessee. Both of his parents had been born in Tennessee and had moved to Dallas in 1871. His parents were devout Episcopalians, and Dad grew up in the Church of the Incarnation in Dallas, which his father and mother helped to found. When he graduated from high school, he won the bishop's scholarship to Sewanee. Sewanee is an Episcopal college and seminary, and Dad's entrance there was seen by everyone as his first step toward the ministry. It was. But it was to be a strange ministry. The first call my father heard was not to serve the Episcopal Church, but to serve the workers and the children of the workers of the Dallas cotton mills.

The man who had the greatest influence on my

father's life was William P. Trent, an English professor at Sewanee. Trent and another professor,
Benjamin Wells, inspired Dad to pursue learning as
few men ever do. They started him reading avidly,
and he never stopped. They also urged him to enter
a national competition in which he won a graduate
scholarship at Harvard. Trent achieved some re-
nown as an English critic and essayist and completed
his teaching career at Columbia. John Erskine, who
had Trent for a professor at Columbia, remembers
him as "a tall Virginian, lank and bearded, full of
courtesy and humor. He became at once a beloved
figure on the campus, all the more attractive because of more than one resemblance to Don Quixote."

In the years at Sewanee, Dad saw much of William Trent and his wife, for she frequently had the
somewhat lonely young man from Texas at their
home. Dad thought so much of Trent that when he
had a son, he wanted to name him Trent Edwards.
Mother thwarted him on that, but all of his life he
called me by Trent's Sewanee nickname, "Andy."

Of a lifetime of reading, Tolstoi and the English
Book of Common Prayer affected Dad most. The
Book of Common Prayer was familiar from the Episcopal service. Trent started him on Tolstoi. The
vivid picture of man's inhumanity to man that Dad
found in Tolstoi's novels and tracts became his
deepest life concern.

At Sewanee he found gaping holes in the religious beliefs that had sent him there, and he was

able to see little relationship between the church of his day and the social mission that called him.

There were political results from the eye opening that Trent (plus Tolstoi) began. For the moment, however, it is sufficient to note that Dad's closest parallel to the toiling and oppressed masses of Czarist Russia were the south Dallas cotton-mill workers. Dad returned to Dallas from Sewanee and Harvard in 1901 and went to live in the cotton-mill district. The shotgun houses, the long hours, the squalor of the lives of the cotton-mill workers outraged him. So did working small children in the mill instead of sending them to school.

In 1903 my father wrote a letter to the *New York Evening Post,* answering a pro-child-labor article that had asserted that children were better off in cotton mills than they had been on the farm. Dad was quite specific about the Dallas cotton-mill problems:

> The cotton mill in Dallas, Tex., whose president is Theophilus King of Boston, whose manager is J. T. Howard of Dallas, and whose superintendent is H. W. Fairbanks of Dallas, works children of eleven and twelve from six-thirty in the morning to six-thirty at night, and, whenever, it suits the management, to nine-thirty at night. . . . In the mill the work is intense, unvarying, and mechanical; and it lasts for twelve or fifteen hours in atmosphere made foul by the breath and sweat of scores of operatives and filled with the fine lint of cotton. . . . The mill has no vacation and no quiet season at all. The operatives are free only after six-

thirty or nine-thirty of each day. When their hours are such as those the chance that children have of learning even to read and to write are far worse than they were in the country. . . . The mill regularly works the mother and the older sisters, and there is no home for the factory family; there is merely a place to eat and to sleep; and some of these hovels here in Dallas, managed by the mill, are almost inconceivably crowded, wretched, and filthy. On the days when the mill does not run at night, the children hurry home at six-thirty, gobble down their food, and then take to the streets, seeking the electric light and the saloon corner as a relief after the monotony of the mill and the misery of their home.

Dad knew Mr. Howard and Mr. Fairbanks personally. In his diary he expressed great surprise at their anger about the *Post* publication when he next visited them at the mill. Dad apparently considered his letter a plain statement of simple truth that should offend no one.

He did, however, find a completely kindred spirit in Dean Hudson Stuck of St. Matthew's Cathedral. At about the same time, Dean Stuck was trying to develop a small mission church and school in the area. Together they drafted and worked for a Texas child-labor law. A child-labor bill was passed, but typically it had been amended and watered down to such an extent that Dad took no joy in its passage.

Then with Stuck furnishing the building and Dad the teaching, Dallas's first night school was

started. Dad went from door to door to talk to the
mill workers and their wives about the school.
Many said that "workin'" from sun to sun made
them just "too tar'd." But about thirty indicated
they would like some "larnin'." The students
ranged from boys of nine or ten to men and women
old enough to be (or who actually were) their
parents. The lint in the mills was such that tobacco
was chewed by nearly everybody who worked
there. All of the students brought their coffee cans
with them into which they spat tobacco juice. Dad
told about seeing children nine years old and up
walk in, set their coffee cans down beside them, and
carefully aim the juice at the can when they needed
to expectorate. After the class, they politely lined
the coffee cans up on the window sills until the next
class.

Dad taught that school in Stuck's mission
schoolroom five nights a week all that year. By the
end of the year many could spell out some words in
the newspaper and could write their names.

Armed with proof of success, Dad went to the
superintendent of schools, J. L. Long, and made
him see the vision of a school for working people to
combat illiteracy. Long agreed to assign a couple of
the best elementary-school teachers in the Dallas
system to the experiment. With Miss Affie Johnson
and Miss Alice Osmund teaching, in 1902 the
Dallas Public Night School was launched.

For a decade Dad lived among the cotton-mill
workers. When he married he brought his bride

with him to the mill district. Dad was elected to the Dallas City Charter Commission from that area, and helped write the Dallas Charter of 1907. Both Mother and Dad taught in the public schools. In addition to all this (and fighting against child labor and volunteer teaching of cotton-mill workers at night), Dad published and edited a weekly labor paper— the first official paper of the Texas State Federation of Labor and the Dallas Trades Assembly.

For a house organ, the *Laborer* was a lively publication. It not only covered the lodge meetings and the convention news of the struggling craft unions that then made up the Texas labor movement, it also covered such topics as: fifty working men in the British Parliament; women's suffrage in Russia; municipal ownership in Catania, Italy; New Zealand, a model commonwealth with no unemployment; and the youth of Count Leo Tolstoi.

The *Laborer* was written for a readership consisting largely of white building tradesmen. In this setting Dad's editorial of April 24, 1909, "For Justice to the Negro and Ourselves," is all the more remarkable:

[T]he treatment meted out to alleged criminals of the Negro race here in Texas is a present disgrace and a future promise of evil. The other day a Negro was burned in Rockwall County, and because another Negro ran from the barbarous mob, he was shot down like a rabbit. A little later on a Negro was arrested at Dawson charged with sending an insulting note to a white woman. Upon learning that there was no law by which this could be punished, a mob took the alleged insulter out and mur-

dered him. At Paris, Texas, yesterday a local of the
Farmers' Union passed resolutions demanding that an
amendment be submitted by which Negroes be allowed
only such schools as their proportion of the taxes would
pay—that is practically no schools at all.

This is a mournful record and it does not begin to be a
complete one. Against it protests every instinct of civilization that has led us in our long march from barbarism to
present-day theoretical humanity. . . .

Every time a Negro is treated with brutal violence,
the mob itself is brutalized. Every time race hatred is
stirred, the Southern labor problem is made worse. And
every effort to hinder Negro education, keep him down
to a wretched ignorance, is but a scheme that will help
pull us down by subjecting us to a sort of labor competition almost if not quite as bad as slavery. And slavery was
a curse to the poor white man of the South as truly as it
was a curse to the Negro. Let us not be deceived. The
fruits of hatred, brutality and violence are violence, brutality and hatred. If we wish justice and peace, we must
provide peace and justice for all.

In these years, also, Dad became one of the best-
known teachers in the Dallas schools. He taught
Latin and algebra. He also coached the high-school
football team and sponsored the debating club. He
inspired a corps of students, many of whom became
his devoted admirers for a lifetime. One of them,
Olin Travis, one of the leading artists in the Southwest, attributes to him the no mean accomplishment of making Latin vitally interesting to his
students. Travis remembers that in teaching Caesar,
Dad compared the corruption in the Roman Empire
to conditions in the city council of Dallas in the first
decade of this century. This may help explain how

Dad also became a central figure in two Dallas school board elections. When his side lost in the last of these in 1908, he was discharged, and he turned to the study and the practice of law.

It was a fairly simple process in 1908 to become a lawyer. A prospective lawyer could be admitted to practice in Texas by passing the bar examination after studying law under the supervision of a lawyer and in the latter's office.

Dad's father, William Mecklen Edwards, was a practicing lawyer in Dallas. He had studied law at Columbia, Tennessee, while living with an uncle, A. O. P. Nicholson, who was chief justice of the Supreme Court of Tennessee. After some lean practice in Hickman County, Tennessee, he and his family came to Dallas, where Dad was born. By 1908 the Edwards family was well known in Dallas, and William Mecklen Edwards was an elected justice of the peace—a considerably more prestigious office then than it is now. Dad read law in his father's office, and by 1910 there was a firm of Edwards and Edwards in the Dallas bar.

While all this might sound like material progress, the early years of Mother and Dad's married life had been hard ones. Two daughters had been born to the young couple while they were sharing the housing, the food, and the long hours of the cotton-mill workers. These two daughters died in infancy of ileitis—dysentery. By the time my sister Nicky and I were born, both Mother and Dad were suffering from tuberculosis, a disease which was to hospitalize them for a long period. How much of all this represented cause and effect we'll never know. But I do know that my mother always blamed the loss of her two babies and the tuberculosis upon the privations of the south Dallas days.

Dad's call to the ministry of the cotton-mill workers had a profound effect on his family and on his long life in Dallas. But so, too, did one of his first cases in the Dallas County courts.

DAD'S FIRST
CRIMINAL CASE

SHORTLY AFTER being admitted to the bar, on March 3, 1910, at 9:30 A.M., Dad was assigned his first criminal case. The circumstances were not auspicious. His client was Allen Brooks, an elderly Negro man. He was charged with criminal assault upon a three-year-old white child. On the morning of the trial one of the lawyers assigned to defend Brooks sent word to the trial judge that he was too ill to appear, and Dad was appointed in his place.

Brooks had been arrested on February 23, 1910, just one week before the trial. Public authorities had had ample warning of trouble. On the night of the arrest a mob surrounded the county jail and threatened to storm it. The sheriff had agreed to let a committee of seven—the six mob leaders and the father of the child alleged to have been attacked—search the jail for Brooks. Brooks was not there, and the mob disbanded.

The day before the trial was to take place, the newspapers ran stories making short shrift of the presumption of Brooks's innocence and announcing when and where Brooks would be the next day.

The following morning, as court convened, the mob was already on hand. Brooks had been brought to the courthouse early and had been taken under guard to the jury room off Judge Seay's courtroom on the second floor. The second floor had been roped off, and fifty sheriff's deputies with twenty Dallas police were on hand. Several times the mob attempted to get up the stairs and was pushed back. On one occasion another judge, E. B. Muse, made a speech to the mob asking that the law be allowed to take its course.

Neither of Brooks's appointed lawyers had ever had a chance to talk to him. When the case was called, Dad and his co-counsel asked for a continuance to prepare for Brooks's defense. Judge Seay gave them one hour in which to interview the prisoner. The lawyers were told that they could see Brooks in the nearby jury room where he was being held under guard. As the two lawyers made their way to the jury room, the mob burst through the first-floor police lines, ran up the stairs to the second floor, and broke into the courtroom—all without a shot being fired.

Dad and his co-counsel got to one door of the jury room just as the mob broke into the other. He never got to the prisoner, who was under guard at the other side of the room. A redheaded deputy who was on guard pulled out his pistol, pointed it up in the air, and shouted, "Stand back!" The mob pushed him aside, seized the prisoner, tied a rope around his neck, and threw the rope out the window

to the crowd outside. Brooks was pulled by the neck
out of the second-story window, falling head first to
the ground below.

Although my father plainly didn't see it that
way, the *Dallas Times Herald* account, printed the
day of the lynching, called the encounter between
the mob and the sheriff's men "a magnificent contest." No words of mine could capture the mood of
that day as did the *Times Herald* story of the lynching:

Rope Placed About Neck.

The sight of their prey seemed to infuriate
the mob that had fought from the first-story to
the jury room. A determined rush was made,
the prisoner was secured, a rope was placed
around his neck and he was pushed out a window to the howling thousands below.

It was finished, but the officers of the law
had made a glorious defense. Each and every
member of the force deserves a medal for they
fought against odds of one hundred to one,
conducted themselves cooly and were at all
times ready to respond to the order of their
superior officer. The police ably assisted their
brother officers. For a time it was hoped that
the fire department could be brought to play
streams of water on the crowd, but the assistance came too late.

It was exactly 11:15 o'clock when the window on the southwest side of the witness room
was thrown open and the surging mob in the
streets caught the first glimpse of the trembling wretch. When they did spy him there
was a cheer went up which could have been
heard for a mile.

A large man with a big white hat was standing immediately under this window and in
response to cries from those who had charge of
the negro in the room the rope was thrown up
to them. Several officers who were in the room
fought desperately to prevent the rope from
being placed about the neck of the trembling
wretch.

Efforts Were in Vain.

Their efforts were in vain, however, and
they were overpowered by numbers. As soon
as the rope was placed around the neck of the
trembling negro, willing hands grabbed hold
and he was jerked out of the hands of the mob
and officers who were trying their best to save
him.

He fell headlong from the window with
arms and legs outstretched and landed on his
head with a thud that could be heard above the
shouting of the mob. The negro's body had no
sooner struck the ground than forty or fifty
men grabbed hold of the rope and with cries of
'to the Elk's arch,' they dragged the form of the
negro around the south side of the courthouse
and up Main street towards Akard.

Went a Dog Trot.

From the time the mob started out with the
negro until the arch was reached they went at
a dog trot and the distance of six blocks or
more was covered in less than five minutes.
No sooner had Akard street been reached
when a young man climbed the telephone
pole at the southeast corner as far as the awn-
ing in front of the Rock Island ticket office and
passed the rope over one of the spikes of the
pole and the body of the negro was dragged up

far enough for the mob to get a view of the form.

Was Dead When Hanged.

That life had already left the body of the negro before he was hanged is the opinion of all. It is believed that the negro's neck was broken and his skull also appeared to have been fractured by the fall. Besides if he had not been killed by the fall he was undoubtedly dead by the time the arch was reached as he was dragged all this distance with the rope drawn tightly around his neck and over the brick pavement. Following those who had hold of the rope was a shouting mob of thousands and there were cheers of exultation all along the route.

The next morning, the *Dallas Morning News* reported that Brooks's shoes and pants were torn from his body as he was dragged by the neck over the cobblestone pavement of Main Street, and that the mob cut his flannel shirt into bits for souvenirs. When the body was cut down, the mob did the same with the rope by which Brooks had been hung.

Much of the newspaper comment after the lynching was devoted to denials by the sheriff (and other officers) that his men had ever drawn their guns. There were also repeated statements from law-enforcement officials that they had been unable to recognize any members of the mob. Both the *Times Herald* and the *Morning News* reported the presence of many "country men" with broad-brimmed hats. Both papers also reported "Negroes" in leadership roles as the lynch mob broke into the jury room—a phenomenon my father never mentioned to me. Sheriff Ledbetter issued a statement to the *Dallas Times Herald,* saying in part: "It was an opportunity for a great deal of bloodshed and it is indeed gratifying to know that none were injured."

The *Dallas Times Herald* reported the next day that it had printed a "record breaking" 28,756 copies on March 3. It also printed a strange interview with the trial judge: "You know, there are some people who will crack a joke under any circumstances," said Judge Seay reminiscently. "Yesterday some lawyer asked me, 'Judge, what are you going to enter on the docket?' I replied that I hadn't decided. He then suggested that I enter, 'The venue has been changed.' Judge Seay was relating his experiences, and this incident seemed to strike those present as decidedly humorous."

Most comment, editorial and otherwise, after the lynching treated the lynch mob much as if it had been a flood, a forest fire, or other act of God. Some editorializing suggested that the real blame lay with the law and the courts for not meting out swift enough justice.

The only outright condemnation of the mob and those who failed to suppress it was in the *Laborer,* the weekly labor paper that my father was still publishing. In a signed editorial Dad said:

> A mob of frenzied barbarians in broad day ran over forty or fifty deputies under the command of a sheriff who was thinking more about

his chances for re-election than his sworn
duty. They broke through the criminal court
room with court in session. They burst into the
jury room and attacked a defendant, who whatever he had done in the past, was at that time
in the alleged protection of the law. They
seized a miserable negro, tied a rope around
his neck and threw him from the second story
of the "temple of justice" (God save the mark!)
of the State of Texas, in the county of Dallas.
They kicked and stamped upon his senseless
body and then dragged it for a quarter of a mile
up the main street of this metropolis of the
Southwest and hanged the naked and bleeding corpse under the most prominent and
pompous monuments of the plutocracy of this
city. . . .

From rumor and hearsay—for no other sort
of investigation was allowed—it appears that
this negro was a diseased degenerate, that he
had been struck on the head years ago and had
never recovered, that there was a soft spot in
his skull as big as two silver dollars, and that
he was within two years of seventy years old.
. . . I shall never believe that civilized criminal procedure would have condemned him to
death as being *sane* before competent physi-
cians had examined him and had stated that he
was sane. . . .

Having been judged *sane,* and then proven
guilty; a civilized society would then have
tried to dispose of the accused in such a man-
ner as absolutely to prevent him from commit-
ting that crime again and as far as possible,
to prevent *any other man.*

But if he had been judged *insane,* a civilized people would have hanged him just as
soon as, and no sooner than, they hang the in-
mates of the insane asylum at Terrell.

FIRST MEMORIES

THE EVENTS I have just described took place before I was born. I learned of them from family legend and some research. My life with Father did not actually begin until four years after I was born in 1914.

Dad's ministry to the cotton-mill workers had taken a heavy toll on my parents. As noted, they lost their first two children, and Mother always blamed the hardships of the first dozen years of their marriage for the loss. In addition, by 1915 both Dad and Mother had developed serious cases of tuberculosis. Both were hospitalized in a t.b. sanitarium at Carlsbad in west Texas—Dad for a year and a half, and Mother for over two years. While Mother and Dad were away, my sister Nicky and I lived in alternating six-month periods with two of our aunts.

My first memory of my father concerns a railroad trip. This was shortly after Dad's return from the t.b. hospital at Carlsbad. We were going back to Dallas from Wilmette, Illinois, where Nicky and I lived with our much-loved Aunt Agnes and her four daughters during the summer half of these years. I was about four. We were in an almost empty Pullman car. It was evening; Dad was reading. The conductor had just come through and turned on all of the lights in the car. When he went on to the car ahead, I proceeded to climb on each unoccupied seat and turn the same lights off. I had just completed this mission of mischief and sat down beside my father again when the conductor came back into our car. He paused and glared at me (or so I thought). Overriding my panic was an unaccustomed sense of security in having a father handy. The conductor didn't say a word. He just turned all the lights back on and left. Dad gave no sign that he noticed the matter—although somehow I felt sure that he had.

During winter months of this period Nicky and I lived in Dallas with our Aunt Bessie and her two daughters. It was there that I first met my mother. She had just come back from the sanitarium at Carlsbad and was still convalescent. I am not quite sure that I knew what a mother was.

When this lady with the pleasant face came into the room and made for me, I let myself be hugged and kissed. Since I felt a little of such activity went a long way, I declined her next invitation to come and sit on her lap. Thereupon Aunt Bessie summoned me to come and sit on her lap. Hers was the accustomed voice of authority and I dutifully went and did so. Aunt Bessie then said, "See, Octavia, he's my boy now. Maybe you better just leave him with me for keeps." Unaccountably the pretty lady burst into tears and ran out of the room.

Aunt Bessie was my father's sister, and I don't think there had ever been much affection between

her and my mother. But I know that whatever there
had been died that day.

Mother had a will of her own. She never came
back to Aunt Bessie's. For a number of months
while she was still recuperating, my sister and I
were taken two hours a day to the apartment a few
blocks away where Mother and Dad were living.
Mother read to us, talked to us, played games with
us. We came to love the visits. Then finally came
the day when we all went home to the house on
Shelby Street in North Dallas where I had been
born. Whatever lack of maternal care there may
have been now was made up for in abundance.

I never thought of Mother in terms of events or
ideas. And since, as time went on, I became so very
much interested in both, I fear for many years I took
her too much for granted.

But Mother was very much a person in her own
right. She was born near Marshall, Texas. In the aftermath of the Civil War, her father, Henry P.
Nichols, had acquired a Texas bride and the plantation she had inherited. It was a heavily mortgaged,
thoroughly run-down cotton farm. Major Nichols
was an authentic Civil War hero—on the Union
side. He had been brevetted major by President
Lincoln after the Battle of Petersburg. Whatever his
military achievements, the attempt at cotton farming was disastrous. The plantation was foreclosed,
and Major Nichols took his wife and brood of five
small children farther west to the banks of the Trinity River and the then small city of Dallas.

The Nichols family settled in the same neighborhood in Dallas where Dad lived. As children Mother and Dad went to the same schools. When Mother showed promise as a student, an older brother and sister saw to it that she went to the University of Texas at Austin and got the chance to graduate in one of the first classes that admitted women.

In 1903 when Mother came back to Dallas from the University of Texas, she and Dad were teaching in the same high school. They soon became engaged. They expected and received the approval of both of their families. However, the welcome Dad's mother gave her daughter-in-law-to-be was not entirely congratulatory. "Oh, Octavia," she said, "I had always dreamed you might marry one of my boys. But never George. I'm afraid he may break your heart. He'll give the shirt off his back to anybody who needs it."

No warning was going to dissuade either party. They had many common interests, and they were in love. They were married in 1905. It was the mating of the eagle and the dove.

Mother was a continuing presence of love in our home. She saw less evil in the world around her than Dad did in the world in which he lived. But she idolized, supported, and sustained her husband. I know now that without her love and help, he could not have been what he was.

Like Dad, Mother was a gifted teacher, and when our family was reunited, she had only two

children to be concerned about. Since disease had
taken her first two children, Mother was desperately determined that she would not lose another.
Precaution was her watchword. The net result was
that if I sneezed, I was promptly put to bed. This
was consistent with the pampering and protecting I
had received from my aunts. My earliest memories
of existence came from a totally female society. My
uncles had been distant figures. Now, however,
there was a father in the house—omnipresent and
all powerful in my eyes. In my new home there was
a strange concept called "courage." Dad talked and
read stories and sang songs about brave men and
brave deeds.

Sundays after dinner he would sit down at the
piano and lead us in singing "Onward, Christian
Soldiers," "Battle Hymn of the Republic," "The
Marseillaise," and "The People's Flag." All these
songs and stories were stirring, and all seemed to
have something to do with courage. So did the poetry he read us and had us learn. I learned to recite
"Incident of the French Camp" and "The Wreck of
the Hesperus." The boy who brought Napoleon the
news about his victory at Ratisbon was certainly
brave enough as "smiling [he] fell dead." I had
some doubt, however, that with my "breast all but
shot in two," I could have managed the sentence,
"Emperor, by God's grace we've got you Ratisbon."
As for the skipper and his daughter on the schooner
Hesperus, I definitely would have preferred to try
heroism in warmer weather.

Then there was the verse that seemed to be my father's favorite:

> *Out of the night that covers me,*
> *Black as the Pit from pole to pole,*
> *I thank whatever Gods may be*
> *For my unconquerable soul.*
>   —William Ernest Henley, "Invictus"

The worst of it was that Dad's message was none too clear to me. Courage in the boy's world of Shelby Street and Sam Houston School was a headlong tackle in football or readiness to fight. Dad's courage seemed to be different. It had nothing to do with either fighting or football. He didn't prohibit my doing either. I knew that he had played football at college and had coached it at Dallas High School. He taught Nicky and me how to swim, play tennis, and play baseball. But he never taught or talked about football or boxing, let alone fighting.

And, into the bargain, as I began to read, all the books I read that were about heroes and bravery were also about wars. And Dad was opposed to war. I was aware that my family's standards were difficult ones.

I am not suggesting that I articulated all these thoughts at age four or, for that matter, at any time during my boyhood. But I was certainly puzzled by my new life and my role in it.

Our house was in a neighborhood called Oak Lawn on what was then the northern outskirts of Dallas. It was a new subdivision of single homes, with many vacant fields. It was then about as

typically middle class a neighborhood as Dallas af-
forded.

Some might remember Oak Lawn in that decade
as not only typically middle class, but also very dull.
That is not the way I remember it. There were boys
for baseball and shinny and rubber guns. There
were always new houses being built, and caves and
scrap houses for us to build. We had a hackberry
tree in the front yard and a fenced-in back yard,
complete with a dog and a once-a-week wash-
woman. A block away, on Maple Avenue, was Park-
land Hospital, the emergency hospital for Dallas.
There were horse-drawn ice wagons, and milk
wagons, and horse-drawn fire engines from the fire
station five blocks north. In time the North Dallas
neighborhood produced a fatal boiler explosion,
numerous fires and accidents, a double murder,
a police raid on a nearby bootlegging operation, and
a dead cat. At most of these I was simply a curious
onlooker, but the dead cat and the double murder
made lasting impressions.

One of the things that impressed me about my
father as I was growing up was that he read Latin
and Greek for pleasure. He had been a teacher. He
was a lawyer. He always brought books and briefs
home at night, carrying them in a green bag, which
in time I came to know as a product peculiar to Harvard University. To my memory it was his only af-
fectation. But to Dallas, Texas, in the 1920s the
green bag was perhaps his least important peculiar-
ity. In that then small, very southern city, close to

the western frontier, he was *the* labor lawyer, *the* ACLU lawyer, *the* NAACP lawyer. Into the bargain, he was anti-Ku Klux Klan, pro-Prohibition, and politically a socialist.

All of this, of course, I learned later. But very early I discovered that my father retired to his big Morris chair in the living room after dinner and read and studied—and that things like broken steps, blown fuses, and dead cats were not in his orbit. They were my mother's concern. But she, too, had been a teacher and had an unfortunate tendency to hammer her fingers as often as the nail.

I inherited fix-it jobs—and the dead cat. First it was just a smell in the general area of the bathroom. It caused some cleaning operations, but in a day or so the smell had grown considerably. By now we were convinced that the odor came from under the house—a dark crawl space that could be entered only on hands and knees. The Texas houses of that day were built on cedar posts, without basements. The sewer and water pipes all ran under the floors in the crawl space. If the sewer pipe had burst, it had to be obvious to anyone who entered the crawl space. I received the assignment to find out. I was about six years old, and I was certainly not expected to do anything more than look to see what the trouble was.

It was a summer day with the Texas sun at its hottest. There was an entrance to the crawl space not far from our back door. It led into the dark, dank area below the house. It was eerie there. Even I had to crawl on hands and knees. If I lifted my head, I struck a floor joist or a water pipe. Previous explorations there had been brief and forbidding. But what I had done once, I thought I could do again.

I had no trouble removing the door. I took a deep breath, held it, crawled in toward where I knew the bathroom plumbing stacks were, and took another breath. The stench hit me. I gasped, nearly vomited, half-rose, hit my head on a joist, and scuttled backward out the trap door into sunlight and breathable air. As I lay doubled up, gasping and fighting nausea, impressions from what I had seen under the house began to come back. I knew that what had overwhelmed me was not sewage; it was something dead.

There were two small vents toward the front of the house. By their light I had seen something on beyond the sewer stacks—a formless shape up against the side of the house. I had to go back to find out. This time I took a deeper breath before I started in. Before I had to breathe again I had crawled half the distance, and there was the problem. It was a big, gray cat. Its eyes were wide open. Its mouth was frozen in what looked like a snarl of defiance. I had never seen a dead animal before. And its tail was only two or three yards from my hand. I could just barely reach and grab it before I had to breathe—but I also knew if I did, I would be very sick. I turned around and crawled as fast as I could go for the trap door. The light and fresh air in front of me helped this time to offset the stench that

I had finally had to gulp in before I could escape out the door.

As soon as I could get my breath, I went to the toolbox that I had been given for Christmas and got a pair of pliers. I had rejected ever touching any part of that cat, but with the pliers I could get it by the tail and drag it. This time I took a long time in the open air before I went back into the crawl space. Crablike, I scuttled as fast toward the cat as I had from him. I reached him without breathing, grabbed the tail with the pliers, and pulled. He followed easily enough, but I couldn't turn around and I had to breathe. I did and dropped the cat and the pliers and fled. The nausea this time was as bad as after the first trip, but the cat was several yards closer to the crawl-space door than it had been. And I knew I could complete the job.

It took two more trips, but ultimately I carried the cat out to the garbage can. Mother was pleased with me, and she mentioned the matter at the dinner table that night. My father said, "So that's what it was. It's a good thing we did not call the plumber."

From Dad's reaction, I guessed that the eerie darkness under the house was not quite "black as the Pit from pole to pole" and that my soul had to watch out for other tests.

The double murder was on Lemmon Avenue, seven blocks away from our house. It took place some years later. A butcher and his wife lived in a second-story apartment over the store where he worked. After some marital difficulties, the butcher caught his wife and another man in bed together in the apartment and shot them both to death with a shotgun. Another boy and I, having heard of the shooting, rode up to view the premises. To our surprise and shock, we found no one at the apartment, the door wide open, and the blood-soaked bed in plain view. The butcher was never indicted.

Talking about this episode at the dinner table one evening, Dad explained that the Texas criminal code provided that when a husband killed his wife and her paramour in bed, it was termed justifiable homicide. But he also added that no such generous provision was made in relation to a wife who undertook the same measures in the same circumstances.

This law remained in effect in Texas until January 1, 1974, when it was repealed by a new penal code.

A SOMEWHAT DIFFERENT FAMILY

MY FAMILY, to all appearances, was quite ordinary. There were four of us—and a dog. We lived in an unexceptional house on an unexceptional street in an unexceptional neighborhood in unexceptional circumstances. My father loved my mother, and she loved him. They both loved their daughter and son, and when we thought of it, we loved them.

In the late afternoons Nicky and I, bathed and dressed for dinner, would sit on the front steps waiting for Dad to come walking home from the end of the streetcar line. When we spotted him, we would race to see who got there first. The winner got to climb on his shoulders and ride astride, triumphantly to the house. The loser got the privilege of carrying the green bag. Mother would greet the three of us as we got to the front door. Anyone watching the scene might have decided "typical American family." With all this, there were differences.

In my earliest days on Shelby Street I slept in a small iron bed. At the foot of it on the wall was a framed inscription. The first letter of each word was illuminated. The words read, "They say—What say they—Let them say." I don't recall anyone ever discussing that inscription. It was a long time before I knew that it was an old English saying which was carved into George Bernard Shaw's mantel. But the message spoke for itself.

Most of the messages did likewise. Dad's favorite comment on the *Dallas Morning News*, for example, was, "I always believe the dateline."

When we shopped for a Christmas present for him, if it was an article of clothing, it had to have a union label—not an easy item to come by in open-shop Dallas.

One of Dad's standard jokes was that "Sic semper tyrannis" means "Take your foot off my neck." (One day, without thinking, I gave that rather free translation in school.) Another of his liberties with Latin (which he loved) was "De gustibus non disputandum est"—to which he always added, "as the old lady said when she kissed the cow."

Dad's favorite phrase for major or minor difficulty was "Toujours l'audace." I knew that meant something like "courage always" long before I ever took any French or knew what courage was. By the time I read *Don Quixote*, I was old enough to find it a little embarrassing that the Don used what I had come to consider our family's slogan when he was charging windmills. Most of Dad's critics would have enjoyed the parallel—if they had known *Don Quixote*.

Another of Dad's favorite adages that he used as a comment on some adversity facing the more impoverished of his clientele was, "Poor folks have poor ways." When the facts seemed to him to justify it, he would add the corollary, "and rich folks have mean ones."

The first political campaign that I remember was in 1924 when Robert La Follette and Burton K. Wheeler ran for president and vice president on the Progressive party ticket. Our house was full of their campaign leaflets and buttons. I was ten and enthusiastic enough to fall off the back fence while engaged in a heated argument with Jimmy Parker over the merits of our respective candidates.

Dad always carried with him something that he was reading, and whenever he had to wait for a few minutes, he used the time to continue. Mother used to say that if he was ever held up, he would pull the *Nation* out of his pocket and start to read while the robber was going through his pockets.

Reading was Dad's sole avocation; and to a considerable degree it was that of his family also. Each member always had a book on a table somewhere that he or she was reading. Books dominated our home. They lined the walls of every room. Dad had read them all; Mother had read many; and Nicky and I each had a bookcase of our own favorites.

Partly by example, and partly by chance, I read omnivorously until I was eleven years old. During those early years I was ill a great deal—or so Mother thought—and I missed about one third of each year

during grammar school. Mother and Dad had read
to me a great deal before I could read. Mother had
taught me to read before I went to school (a fact that
my first-grade teacher at Sam Houston School had
not particularly appreciated). Dad selected and
brought me books.

No one could have had a more landlocked
boyhood than I did in central Texas, but between
illness and books, I traveled the seas of the world.
The top of our hackberry tree became the main-
top—the crow's nest—of all the famous ships in
literature. I was there at dizzying heights above
the deck and ocean—with Peter Simple, Midship-
man Easy, Masterman Ready, Richard Henry Dana
in *Two Years before the Mast,* and the heroes of
Kingsley's *Westward Ho!*

What I read wasn't all great literature by any
means. It included countless Tom Swift stories. But
over and above the sea stories (I read all of Marryat,
and I think all of Conrad), I also read all of Scott and
Dickens, Arthur Conan Doyle and Mark Twain.
Many days when I was sick I would read three
complete books, and my father had to add to his
usual day at his law office a stop by the public
library to return those finished and pick up a new
supply.

Dad's library trips started me on Joseph P.
Altshelter. I read every available one of Altshelter's
nearly endless series of Civil War novels. The
Dallas of my boyhood was a small southern city.
The saga of the Confederacy was a basic part of its

culture. Though I knew early that my father and mother had very different views on many topics than those I heard everywhere else, no one sought to diminish my joy at the gallantry of Lee and Stonewall Jackson and Jeb Stuart and their men as they won such famous victories as Shiloh, Vicksburg, and Gettysburg. At least that was the way I understood what Altshelter wrote. Later I was to be considerably puzzled by the fact—noted not too conspicuously in my grammar-school history—that the North, after all the Confederate victories, had somehow won the war.

I do remember vividly, however, that toward the end of my Altshelter craze Dad came home one day with Stephen Crane's *The Red Badge of Courage* and told me it was "a great book"—a phrase he rarely used. I read it with more than usual interest and with some continuing sense of surprise. These, too, were brave men fighting for a cause they believed in, and they were on the Union side.

Later Dad gave a similar accolade to Edward Bellamy's *Looking Backward.* Bellamy pictured a peaceful and classless society where men worked according to their abilities and received according to their needs. I had no inclination then to doubt either the practicality of Utopia or the possibility of its early achievement. The small society that I knew best—my family—seemed to function approximately this way.

Like most babies, I had been baptized at birth in the religious faith of my parents. My Episcopalian mother saw to that. In addition, when I was born, my father took out a Socialist party card in my name. He maintained that card for all the years of my minority. I took his political beliefs for mine as readily as most children accept their family's religion. When I began to see the world more particularly through my own eyes, I saw it somethat differently than Dad did. But the convictions that led me to spend my adult political life in the Democratic party of Michigan developed gradually and not out of any searing revolt of son against father.

There were families where the social development of the child was considered more important than school marks. Mine wasn't one of them. In sequence, Es, 90s, and As were expected. My sister preceded me in grammar school, high school, and college, leaving that kind of trail behind her. I wasn't that enthusiastic about the matter. But Dad created a high degree of expectancy, and generally I tried to live up to his standards.

Nicky and I learned early that if there were chores to perform in our household, the only way to postpone or avoid them was to plead for time to finish a chapter in a book or a piece of homework. The latter was sacrosanct.

In grammer school I really didn't deserve too much credit for my marks. All through my periods of sickness at Sam Houston School I had expert tutoring at home, which I was sure was not available to any other student. I think I had the feeling that rehearsing the lesson with a teacher—even if he or she was a parent—was sort of unfair. At eleven, following an emergency operation for appendicitis, the illness that had plagued my boyhood disappeared and I began to experience the good health that has enriched the rest of my life. Along with good health came much greater extracurricular activity.

I found that by working in class, I could eliminate a lot of homework. I was frequently engaged in trying to persuade Dad that I had done my assignments. Somewhat to his frustration, I think, my report cards usually met the family standard. Dad took to referring to my schooling as "education by osmosis." One fact was certain—Dad's standards never varied. Once I brought home a couple of *B*s. It was a grim evening, which I attempted to lighten by pointing out that a *B* was, after all, an above-average grade. Dad's cold reply was, "Son, the average is mighty low."

By the time I was in North Dallas High School, detailed parental supervision had tapered off and I was enmeshed in all sorts of nonacademic activities. Dad, however, greatly wanted me to share his love of Latin. He considered Latin an excellent intellectual exercise and very much a part of our living language.

I took Latin each year at North Dallas. The teacher was a precise and peppery little lady named Mrs. Ethridge. She ran her classroom somewhat like a drill sergeant. She knew exactly what she wanted and expected to get it. She and my father

were in agreement on one thing—I didn't work hard
enough on Latin. Here, against considerable resis-
tance, Dad insisted on having me read the Latin lesson to him every night preceding a Latin class.
There was no good my guessing at translations. He
knew. But he never told me more than that what I
had guessed was wrong. I had to go back, look up
every word, and work it out for myself. The results
were that I liked just about every class in high
school except Latin—and that I represented my
high school in the statewide Latin contest.

Dad believed in "getting started early." I was
entered in grammar school early and graduated
from both high school and college in three years
each. Thinking back on this, I don't remember feeling pushed or ordered. My father was a strong per-
sonality. What he wanted done, those around him
generally sought to do.

We didn't have many family vacations. Several
times in the summer, however, we drove to the
Texas gulf coast. I particularly remember one such
trip to Corpus Christi. We stayed in a cabin in a
resort near the beach, and Corpus for me began a
lifetime of fascination with the southern seas and
their coral beaches.

One day Dad took me to a pier to fish. To my
delight I caught several small fish, which Dad secured by putting his straw hat on them. I remember dancing around one of these catches, which
was flopping loose on the dock dangerously near

the edge and yelling, "Dad, put your hat on him!"

The most vivid recollection of that trip, however, had nothing to do with sea or sand. It had to do with two Italian fishmongers—Sacco and Vanzetti. In my family their names were utterly familiar. My father was completely convinced that they were innocent of the Braintree payroll murders for which they had been sentenced to death. He was also convinced that Massachusetts was determined to execute them, in spite of their innocence.

With the optimism that afflicted me even at that age, I was sure that since they were innocent, something would happen at the last moment to save their lives. Indeed, many things had happened to do so in the past. This time the execution was scheduled for a Tuesday night in Massachusetts. We had no hope of hearing news until the following morning in Corpus Christi.

That morning found Mother, Nicky, Dad, and me in a café fronting on the Gulf of Mexico, ordering breakfast. Dad disappeared to get a paper. I saw him as he came back into the restaurant. His face was taut and gray in color. He hardly needed to tell us. To the four of us it was as if members of the family had died.

SUNDAYS

SUNDAY AFTERNOONS were special times for me. Dad took me on long walks. Sometimes we explored North Dallas—more often the Trinity River bottomland not too far away. We climbed Pole Cat Mountain and poked through the ruins of the original Dallas city waterworks on its top. Pole Cat Mountain in most others states would be a small hill. We visited the new city waterworks and were warmly greeted and shown through it by an engineer who had been one of Dad's clients. We walked around the filtration plant where Trinity River water was stored and made potable. Dad talked about things we saw, about his boyhood, about people he knew, about his cases, about what he believed, about his family. He and his brothers disagreed politically, but he always spoke of them with great affection. On one of these walks he told me this story:

When he first started to practice law in Dallas, it was still a frontier town. Quite a few lawyers carried pistols and occasionally used them. The first year he was admitted to the bar, two lawyers had let it be known around town that they were gunning for each other. They met at the courthouse—each drew and fired—one of them died on the courthouse lawn. The other was neither arrested nor indicted.

Several years later Dad was involved in a trial with a contentious lawyer who had killed several men in similar affairs. On one of the afternoons of the trial Dad and his opposing lawyer got into an argument over a motion and exchanged some strong words. That evening a friend called Dad at home and told him that his opponent had been in a bar-room earlier in the evening saying that if George Clifton Edwards gave him any more trouble at court the next day, he was going to kill him.

Dad said he had a duty to a client and neither had a gun nor any desire to have one. He worried about the matter, but went to court the next day without doing anything about the call. He thought that it was more liquor than actual threat. He got to the court early and sat at the counsel table on his side of the courtroom. As time for convening court came nearer, the courtroom began to fill up and Dad looked back. There, in the front row, just behind the rail, were his four brothers, Pat, Will, Alf, and Walker. Uncle Walker was seated on the end of the bench. It was a hot day but he had an overcoat on and he had his hand in his right overcoat pocket. Obviously somebody had called Walker, too. About that time opposing counsel came in. He, too, took a look around. Dad said he didn't know what his opponent thought, but that he made up his mind right then to be as polite as he knew how.

He said he doubted that the crowd in that courtroom ever saw or heard two lawyers argue a case
more courteously than they did that day.

On one of our walks Dad told me about an incident that obviously had bothered him a good deal.
It happened about 1904 or 1905. He had just returned to Dallas from Sewanee and had started
publishing the *Laborer*. That evening he had written an article for his paper expressing the feeling
that southern men should not abandon the courtesy
of giving up their seats on streetcars to women. That
same night about midnight he was sitting in back of
a crowded streetcar when a woman came in, looking
tired from a long day's work. Dad got up and, as he
put it, "sneaked out of the car" and walked the rest
of the way home. The woman didn't get the seat.
The reason that he hadn't bowed to her and tried
obviously to see to it that she got the seat he was
seeking to give her was that she was Negro.

Doubtless the risk of doing anything more than
he did would have been considerable at midnight
on Saturday in Dallas in 1905. But the episode still
bothered him—twenty years later. He said the
worst part was that he knew better, but he didn't do
better. "Andy," he told me, "black skin does not
take away kinship to God."

On those Sundays we saw the Trinity in its many
stages and moods—from the turbulent flood of
spring to the small quiet stream of summer. On several occasions we walked the 2 miles to the Dallas
city dump. This was several acres of garbage, waste,

and abandoned objects of all sorts, many of them
fascinating to a small boy. The dump had an interest
for Dad, too, since 10 of the acres on which it was
located had been in the Edwards family since 1871.
Dad had driven the family cows to pasture there
during all of his youth. The land still belonged to
the Edwardses, although they had come very near
to losing it. A grandiose and (for many years) unsuccessful Trinity River levee scheme had resulted in
prohibitive assessments on the land. In the Depression the levee district went bankrupt. When it was
reorganized and at the last moment before losing
title, Dad negotiated a settlement of the assessments on the pasture. He and his sister and his
brothers managed to pay the settlement and keep
title to the land. When I saw it, the land was leased
to the city to pay the taxes. Unsightly as the dump
was—to my aunt, uncles, and, to some degree, Dad,
it represented the pot of gold at the foot of the rain-
bow.

In time Dallas grew big enough to create that
pot of gold. But not while any of them were still
alive to share it. A great expressway was built across
that pasture. Nearby was built the Dallas Trade
Mart, where President Kennedy was scheduled to
speak November 22, 1963.

The Edwardses' cow pasture of 1871 saw some
interesting history before it was finally sold (after
Dad's death) for a sum that would indeed have been
a fortune for one person, but was hardly that for the,
by then, many joint heirs.

Dad did achieve some use of the pot of gold, and it was typical of him. In his will he included specific bequests to be paid out of his portion of the sale of the levee property. Among the recipients were the University of the South at Sewanee, Tennessee; Harvard University; the League for Abolition of Capital Punishment; the American Civil Liberties Union; and the National Association for the Advancement of Colored People.

On one Sunday Dad talked about his father. William Mecklen Edwards had been born in North Carolina. He left home in his teens after conflict with a stepfather and followed the trail of the pioneers westward, first to Tennessee and later to Texas. As mentioned earlier, in Columbia, Tennessee, he lived in the home of an uncle, A. O. P. Nicholson, who had been senator from Tennessee and was then chief justice of the Supreme Court of Tennessee.

William Edwards had had an arm shot off in a boyhood hunting accident. As a consequence he was left behind when his brother and other young men from Columbia marched off to join the Confederate army in the Civil War. He was in Columbia while Confederate general Nathan Bedford Forrest made it his headquarters, and was still there when the Union army captured it.

On one occasion Willie came upon a Union deserter who was robbing the Nicholson springhouse. The soldier was so preoccupied with a jug of milk that Willie picked up his rifle, aimed it at the soldier (using one arm and a stump), and proceeded to march him toward Columbia to turn him over to Union headquarters. The soldier began a conversation with Willie, gradually dropped back out of the line of fire from his own rifle, and suddenly reached out and recaptured the gun. Then it was Willie's turn to march.

Under Chief Justice Nicholson's influence, William Edwards studied law, and after the war ended, he started to practice in Hickman County, Tennessee. He married Elva Gray, the daughter of a prosperous farmer, George Washington Gray, whose dislike for being called "Wash" Gray barely prevented my father from being named George Washington also.

Life was hard in Tennessee after the Civil War and in 1871 William, his wife, and their first two children left Tennessee for Texas. Dad quoted his father as saying that he arrived in Dallas one-armed, suffering with asthma, and broke, with a wife and two little boys—but he never regretted the move.

Every second or third Sunday Dad would take me with him to vesper services at St. Matthew's— the Episcopal cathedral. The Church of the Incarnation, which our family generally attended, was too much society and too little social gospel for me. I had quit Sunday school and didn't care much more for the Incarnation adult service. But St. Matthew's was very different. Its dimly lit Gothic nave was vast, beautiful, mysterious. Vesper services usually drew only a handful of people. The organ music and

the familiar hymns echoed in the nearly empty cathedral. We seemed very much alone. The vesper
service itself was simple and full of the sonorous
prose of the King James version of the Bible. Dad
loved the service, and we followed it together in the
prayer book. The sermons were very short and
seemed to me to say more than the much longer
ones at the Incarnation. In spite of the skepticism I
then professed, I think I concluded that if there was
a God, this was a good place for him.

Sunday evenings in front of the fireplace Dad
read to us in those early years. He read all of *The
Swiss Family Robinson,* a chapter a week. I was so
fascinated by it that I could hardly wait for the next
week. Later when Nicky and I could both read, he
changed the format and each of us would read in
turn. At one point we started reading Shakespeare.
Dad assigned each of us two or three characters to
read. We tried as best we could to keep place and
make the dialogue sound like conversation.

MY COUNTRY COUSINS

IN THE TWENTIES cotton was king in Texas. Cotton fields surrounded Dallas on all sides. Our house was near the city limits, only a few blocks from where the cotton farms began. Nonetheless, I would have grown up entirely a city boy if I hadn't had some country cousins relatively close by.

Harry and Walter Crump were my closest friends in these early years. When I was a boy they lived on a farm several miles from Lemmon Avenue. The terminal building for the Dallas' Love Field airport is built on land where the Crump's small farm and house and general store had been. Their mother, who was my first cousin, had been named Octavia after my mother. She was Mother's only niece, and Mother was particularly fond of her. Her husband, Harry, Sr., brought Dad all his legal problems—impressive in number if not in dollars.

Of all our relatives, the Crumps were the simplest, most natural, and least sophisticated. In Texas language they were "real country." They were also the branch of the family with whom we had the warmest relationship.

The Crumps' farmhouse was not prepossessing in appearance, but it glowed with hospitality. Octavia was a big and vital woman who handled her brood of children (and her husband, for that matter) with ease and laughter. She had a wood stove to cook on, an outdoor privy, and no running water. None of this bothered her. When running water and an inside toilet did appear, she welcomed them with enthusiasm. But she kept and defended and swore by the wood stove long after she had an electric one in her kitchen.

Miracles of hospitality were produced on that stove. I was the closest relative and the most frequent visitor. They made it obvious to me that I was always welcome—at any hour and without any notice. With three growing boys and two girls and herself and Harry to feed, Octavia did not seem to mind my additional appetite. I have seen a family of eight drop in just before mealtime with no warning at all, heard Octavia urge them into staying, seen her start the meal from scratch, helped her chase and catch the chickens in the nearby chicken yard, and watched her wring their necks and begin converting them into a platter of crisp, brown fried chicken, bountiful enough to satisfy the largest appetite among her sudden guests. And all of this with laughter and directions to all who were handy. "Lawzy me, Georgie, head off that white one," she would say when we were catching the chickens. Octavia was the only person I can remember (outside of books about the South) who actually and regularly said, "Lawzy me!"

I became a very regular visitor at what my father

called "Crumptown," usually riding the 2½ miles by bicycle.

On my way out Lemmon Avenue, about a quarter of a mile before I got to Crumptown, I passed a settlement called Elm Thicket. It was in the vicinity of Lovers' Lane and Lemmon Avenue. I remember it as a shack town that Negro squatters had built from whatever building materials they had found. In Texas if you settled on, fenced in, and held land against all comers for ten years, you acquired legal title. Many of the settlers in Elm Thicket had thus squatted themselves into title.

Many of the houses were tiny hovels made of scraps of lumber, boxwood, and tar paper. Some had no windows. They were built on small plots, fenced in with even more nondescript materials. Due to numerous children, chickens, and dogs, the yards had no grass. Elm Thicket was a sea of mud in wet weather and a cloud of dust the rest of the year. Poverty was a permanent guest and fire a frequent visitor in Elm Thicket.

Many of Harry Crump's general store customers came from Elm Thicket—and so did many of his credit risks and losses. Elm Thicket provided me with my first real view of Negro life in Dallas. To my eyes it did not have much to recommend it.

Big Harry's main job was the general store. He did very little crop farming. The store, however, did a considerable volume of business, and, as mentioned, Dad was Harry's lawyer. They could hardly have been more different, but Harry spoke of Dad with great respect, and Dad and Mother had great affection for all residents of Crumptown. I believe my family spent more time with the Crumps on week ends and holidays than with any of our other relatives.

While the Crump place was hardly a working farm, there were always cows to milk, chickens to feed, and somebody had to take the slop out to the pigs. Harry, Jr., and Walter had grown up with these chores from babyhood and were quite generous in sharing them with a beginner. Some of a city boy's mysteries concerning life and death were quickly and explicitly answered. The eggs I collected in the hen house and the milk I brought in from the barn went right to the table, as did the meat from the hogs that Big Harry slaughtered and the chickens from Octavia's chicken yard. And after watching the servicing of a mare and the birth of a calf, I had little need (or tolerance) for stories about the birds and the bees.

There was always a horse or two at the place. And Harry and Walter had guns—first BB guns and then .22s. Somehow Mother's safety precautions, which hemmed me in fairly closely on Shelby Street, were waived at Crumptown. I learned to ride a little and got in quite a bit of rifle practice on tin cans and chee chees.

Then there was the horse trough. Big Harry put it in with the thought of feeding cattle for market— something that he never really did on any scale. During the years when I was most frequently at the farm, it was not much used—except by Harry, Jr., Walter, and me. We used it for naval battles.

A naval engagement, of course, called for ships and guns. Our ships were wood-block hulls with sticks for masts and paper sails. The guns, however, were more realistic. They were small muzzle-loading cannons made from copper tubing. We cut an appropriate length, hammered one end of the tube completely closed, and filed a touchhole just ahead of the closure. A pinch of black powder shaken down the tube, a little piece of wadding tamped on top of that, a BB dropped on top of that, another piece of wadding, and with a few grains of black powder on the touchhole for primer, it was ready to be aimed and fired. We mounted the guns on wood-block caissons, and we fired them from the concrete ends of the horse trough at the ships of the enemy fleet floating at the other end. A BB through a paper sail was a hit, and a shot that dismasted a ship meant that it was out of action. Our powder magazine was a two-pound flask of black powder. We played this game for years, day after day, in the summertime. Somehow we never blew ourselves up.

Big Harry Crump was short and stocky. He wore his belt below a rather substantial belly, creating an underslung appearance. Nonetheless, he was a formidable man. The nearby farmers used his general store as their supply center for materials, tools, and whatever food they didn't raise themselves. It served the same purpose for Elm Thicket. In addition, the store was a social and political center.

In many ways Harry Crump was the acknowl-
edged head of a small fiefdom, and he understood
his power. He was hardly an exploiter. Big Harry
worked in that store from sunup frequently to long
after sundown. While his family always had ample
food upon the table, there was little else about their
way of living that represented luxury. Dad, who, of
course, had many opportunities to know, respected
Harry and said that he never tried to overreach anyone. When the Depression hit, Harry was caught
between the suppliers of his store who could collect
from him, and countless numbers of his now jobless
customers to whom he had advanced credit and
from whom he could not collect.

Harry had a ready joke and a ready laugh. I
never heard of his being involved in a fight. With all
this, somehow he gave the impression of being a
man with whom you just wouldn't want to fool
around.

One day, Big Harry was cutting up a side of beef
on the butcher block in the rear of the store. His
knife slipped and almost cut through the index
finger on his left hand. The finger was dangling gro-
tesquely by a bit of flesh. Harry looked at it carefully. He then laid his left hand back on the butcher
block, with the index finger spread out away from
the other fingers, took the butcher knife and se-
vered the finger completely. He flicked it into the
offal barrel with his butcher knife. He went to the
house, bandaged his hand, came back and finished
butchering the side of beef.

On busy days I occasionally helped out in the store. There was usually a buzz of conversation. One day there was a sudden silence. I looked up from whatever I was doing and saw Big Harry face to face across a counter with a very big Negro man—a stranger to me. Each was measuring the other. There was a taut-muscled moment of silence. Then Harry's voice, hard like a whip crack, "Listen, boy, when you speak to me, you call me Mistah Crump." Another segment of silence. Two, three seconds, perhaps. Long enough for me to think of the size and the anger of the Negro man towering over the store owner and of the .38 revolver I knew was within Harry's reach. Then the bigger man's shoulders relaxed in surrender. "Yassuh, Mistah Crump," he said, and I started breathing again. Big Harry turned his back without another word and started filling the big man's order. When he gave him his change, Harry said, "Now, Will, you can come in here, but only if you behave yourself. You understand?" The big Negro picked up the bag of groceries and said, "Yassuh, Mistah Crump, I understand." He walked out the door, and I watched him turn slowly toward Elm Thicket—his shoulders sagged forward and his eyes on the ground.

From the back of the store, where the regulars were gathered, came some colorful profanity.

Harry, Sr., looked at me and (doubtless thinking more about Dad than about me) he said, "Georgie, you give them an inch and they'll take a mile."

During all of my life in Dallas I saw a great deal

of the two boys in that family. Harry and Walter were the closest things to brothers that I ever had.

Somehow, in spite of the Depression, the Crumps managed to send their children to college. When Harry, Jr., graduated, he went to law school and then entered the practice of law. Dad had been the only lawyer he had known well, and frequently early in his practice Harry was in the courtroom watching when Dad was trying a case or arguing a motion. He liked to tell of the incident in which Dad and a rather pompous opponent were arguing a point of law. The other lawyer had brought half a dozen law books to court with him and had quoted from each at some length. When he finished talking about the last case, Dad (who had brought no books to court) arose and advised the court, "Your honor, my brother finally got around to the case which controls the matter before us. The first five cases he talked about have nothing to do with the matter. As to the last case, he read the general rule from page 245. If your honor will just turn the page to page 246, you will see that the court recognized the exact problem we have here in dealing with the first exception to the general rule." At that point Dad sat down. The judge ultimately ruled in his favor on the authority of the exception on page 246.

World War II interrupted young Harry's law career. Like many Texans, Walter Crump volunteered for the Air Force immediately after Pearl Harbor. Harry followed not long thereafter.

On February 8, 1943, Captain Walter Crump was reported missing in action. The B-25 bomber that he piloted was hit by antiaircraft fire in action against Rommel's forces over the North African desert. Several parachutes were seen to open before his plane crashed. Until the war was over and the prisoners of war had all been freed with no word of Walter, his family hoped for his return. We had no hope.

On August 2, 1943, Captain Harry Crump was reported missing in action after the B-24 on which he was navigator failed to return from a raid on the Ploesti oil fields in Romania. His ship had last been seen making its bombing run over the target. Until the last of the war prisoners had been repatriated with no word of Harry, his family hoped for Harry's safe return, and so did we.

A letter from Dad in September, 1944, to my army camp said:

> I have not said anything about it but the Ploesti fields where Harry went down have been in my thoughts daily in reading of the Romanian collapse and the release of some 1400 flyers. But there has been nothing to give us hope against the grim probability that his bomber was just blown to pieces in that first low raid August a year ago. Nor have we anything about Walter.

The difference was not in our attitude toward the two. We were deeply fond of them both. But Walter had been pilot of his ship. The parachutes counted from his plane did not represent the entire

crew. Harry had been navigator on his ship and did
not have the duty of keeping the ship in the air until
all other crew members had jumped.

For either of them shirking any part of what they
knew as duty would, I think, have been impossible.

Few families gave as much to their country in
World War II as did this one. With Harry and Walter
missing in action, a third son went into the service
and, though exempt, sought combat duty. The
only son-in-law led one of the first B-29 strikes on
Tokyo. Dad remarked once that he never heard
Harry or Octavia utter a complaint about their risks
or their losses.

THE NORTH TEXAS BUILDING

THE NORTH TEXAS BUILDING in the 1920s probably housed more trial lawyers than any other building in Dallas. My father's law office was on the fifth floor. Like all such offices, his was equipped with a roll-top desk, a big library table, an overhead fan, many glass-covered bookcases filled with law books, filing cabinets, and a typewriter. Unlike other offices, his had a picture of Eugene V. Debs and one of Norman Thomas, a battered, leather-bound volume of Blackstone's *Commentaries on the Common Law*, a chess set, and an avowed atheist by the name of Richard Potts.

Dick Potts's status in Dad's law office was completely undefined. He was just there—most of the time. The unstated arrangement seemed to be that (when I was not there) he served as a somewhat overage office boy in exchange for a business address and a telephone.

Potts was one of the most interesting characters I ever met. He was a slender, little old man, bald-headed, with a fringe of white hair. He had bright blue eyes and never-failing good humor. He was always ready for an argument about religion, and he was always ready to play chess. I don't know how much he taught me about religion, but he certainly made every effort to teach me to play chess.

Potts was a fervent disciple of Robert Ingersoll, the nineteenth century's leading atheist. He was also the most complete practicing Christian I have ever known. He had no family, lived in a rooming house, and eked out a precarious existence as the editor, publisher, and sole owner of a little magazine called the *Common Herd*. His must have been the simplest publishing business ever. Since Potts both wrote his magazine and sold it personally by hand, after he sold enough copies to pay the printer, the rest was his. He had several hundred more or less regular customers and would make rounds in the downtown area with a dozen copies in his pocket. It did not take many sales a day to give him his daily bread.

The *Common Herd* was against the Dallas establishment generally, but more particularly it was against the Dallas religious establishment. In a town full of fundamentalists, the *Common Herd* examined, dissected, and ridiculed every bit of fundamentalist dogma and quite a few Dallas dogmatists. At times it made rather lively reading.

No preacher I ever met exhibited more zeal in speaking and writing for his faith than Richard Potts did for his nonfaith. It seemed somewhat odd to me that he should belabor the Christian religion so industriously while he practiced its fundamental tenets so doggedly.

I knew him best in the early years of the Great Depression. The issues of the *Common Herd* were more haphazard than usual and Potts's income was equally diminished. But he shared his bounty (such as it was) with all who asked—and there were many. If a man asserted he was hungry, Potts would take him to a restaurant and buy him a meal. One cold February day he came into the office shivering and without his coat. It was a new one that we had urged him to buy to replace one disgracefully old and shabby. He had met a man on the street who was coatless and cold and, into the bargain, had no place to go to get warm. Potts had given him his new coat.

One vivid memory keeps me from characterizing Potts as a strange sort of latter-day saint. His chess game! He was a master of the assassination of the queen by a seemingly inoffensive knight. Over and over he trapped me into bold and nearly devastating moves, only to catch me just short of victory with a pounce on an apparently secure piece and a shout of "checkmate" achieved with the unlikely combination of a bishop (clear across the board), a knight, and a couple of pawns. The glee he exhibited in such a triumph seemed to me to have in it much more of the devil than the saint.

During the summers, I worked in my father's law office. I answered the telephone, and I minded the office when he was out. Frequently I accompanied him to court, to the records building, and, on one unforgettable occasion, to see a client in the Dallas city jail.

We were admitted through a steel-barred door to a large room off the jail office, where my father began interviewing his client through the bars. Shortly, my interest in that interview was abruptly ended by blows followed by screams and groans coming from a small room partitioned off in a corner of the lockup room where we were. A few moments earlier I had seen several men lead a redheaded prisoner, whose arms were handcuffed behind his back, into that room. The sounds of blows and anguish continued for some time. Every few minutes someone went into or came out of that small room. And when the door was open, the scene in the room was unforgettable. A man on each side of a heavy table had the prisoner's arms twisted so that he was bent forward over the table. His ankles were shackled to the table legs so that his legs were spread apart. A big man stood behind him with a length of rubber hose in his hand. The subject was stripped to the waist and long, red welts stood out on the white skin of his back. Then the door would close and the blows and moans would start again.

On several occasions the blows and moans ceased for a time. Then came the most fearsome shriek of pain and terror I had ever heard. On one occasion the door was open when this occurred and I saw the big man who had been wielding the rubber hose reach down between the prisoner's spread-out legs and grab and twist his testicles. Obviously I couldn't see the testicles; but I saw the grab and the twist—and I heard the shriek.

There was a Negro trusty mopping the floor of the lockup room. He kept right on mopping, without a glance toward the little room. Other jail personnel and other prisoners went about their routine jobs inside and outside of the bars without ever looking in the direction of this anguish scene. No one exhibited the slightest concern about the two outsiders who were in the bull-pen area that day. When we left the jail the third degree was still going on.

I profoundly doubt that anyone could stand the torture that I saw being routinely administered to that redheaded prisoner without "confessing" (if that's the right word) to anything the interrogator desired.

Of course, since 1791 the Constitution has read, "No person . . . shall be compelled in any criminal case to be a witness against himself." But it wasn't until 1936—about ten years after the Dallas jail events I have just described—that the Supreme Court decided *Brown* v. *Mississippi*. In it the Supreme Court struck down a conviction based on a confession extracted by alternately beating and hanging a prisoner by the neck until he not only confessed, but did it in the detail desired by his torturers.

My father was a very determined man. He knew that protests at the jail or to the police would have absolutely no effect. The next morning after the third-degree episode, however, he took me with him when he went before the Dallas County grand jury to seek investigation and indictment of the three men we had seen torture the red-headed prisoner. Dad went in first, and when he came out I went in. I told the grand jury just what I have written above. The foreman of the jury asked whether I knew the names of the men in the little room. I said I didn't. The foreman patted me on the head, said I was a fine boy, and gave me an apple. Then the jury voted a "no bill."

I ate the apple. It was a good apple.

Later that day I told my father about my session with the grand jury. (I don't recall anyone telling me that the session was supposed to be secret.) I also told him about the foreman and the apple. He asked me what I did with the apple, and I replied that it was a good apple and I ate it. My uncompromising father replied that he would have thrown it away.

One sequel to Dad's bout with t.b. was a lifetime habit of a nap after lunch. He had a big leather couch in his office. He ate a quick lunch, frequently at Bogan's Market, and then hung a sign on the outside of his office door which said, "Gone to Mexico, back at 1:30." He also cut off the phone—the first episode in a long, if hardly earthshaking, controversy.

For many years Dad stifled the phone during his nap by the simple means of a folded bit of paper wedged between the clapper and the bell. One day a Southwestern Bell repair man told him that he could put in a cut-off switch for $1.80, and Dad told him to do it.

The switch worked fine, and Dad was happy with his bargain until on the following month's bill he noticed a new and separate 8-cent charge. He called the phone company and asked what the 8 cents were for.

"Rental for the cut-off switch" was the reply.

"I bought the switch," said Dad.

"Oh, no, we don't sell them. We only rent them. The one dollar and eighty cents was just a service charge."

"No one told me that," said Dad, "and I won't pay any rental. You can come take it out."

The Bell System removed its switch. Dad went back to his folded-paper noise squelch. Briefly, peace returned.

Dad had paid the offending bill, minus 8 cents. On the following month's bill, he found a notation "arrearage 8¢." He paid the bill, deducting 8 cents. This went on for some time. Then the Southwestern Bell Telephone Company sent him a letter that it was going to cut off his phone service if he didn't pay the 8-cents arrearage. Dad replied by sending a letter notifying them that he was paying under protest and enclosed an 8-cent check, similarly inscribed. Then he sat down and typed out a bill of complaint alleging breach of contract. He also alleged that the rental charge was in violation of state law and cited the statute he relied upon, and that the threat to cut off his phone service when he owed them nothing damaged his professional reputation.

Southwestern Bell lawyers filed no answer but did file a timely motion for extension of time, asserting that the suit required intensive research, since it involved novel and undecided questions of law. They asked Dad to agree to the extension, which, magnanimously, he did. Half a dozen similar extensions were sought, and, with Dad agreeing, were granted by the court. About two years after the filing of the suit, two Southwestern Bell lawyers made an appointment and came to see Dad at his office.

They wanted to talk settlement of the law suit. They approached the problem in a wholly conciliatory fashion by admitting that they had made a mistake both in failing to notify him of the rental charge in advance and in sending the service-cut-off threat. They indicated a willingness to discuss any reasonable settlement figure. Dad said, fine, he would take 8 cents.

The two lawyers laughed, and one said, "Now, Mr. Edwards, we're really serious about wanting to settle this matter. We know we've caused you trouble and we're fully prepared to pay. We don't want to try this law suit. You just name a figure and we will try to come as close to it as we can."

Dad said, "Eight cents."

He finally convinced them that that was what he wanted and they left, happily undertaking to draft a settlement and dismissal stipulation and to accompany it with an 8-cent check within a few days. These documents arrived, Dad signed the stipulation, the suit was dismissed, Dad closed his file, and again peace descended.

About five years later Dad got a call from the same two lawyers, wanting to see him. They didn't want to talk about the problem or even identify it on the phone, and again Dad made an appointment at his office.

This time the opening apologies for the Southwestern Bell's sins against my father were more profuse and utterly puzzling to Dad. The chief spokesman finally said that they had thought the matter had been settled to the satisfaction of everybody—but obviously this wasn't so. What could they do to adjust it? Dad said that he was completely satisfied and had long since forgotten about it.

At which point the Bell lawyer said, "But Mr. Edwards, you have never cashed that check and the Southwestern Bell books have been eight cents out of balance for five years."

This time it was Dad's turn for apologies, which grew more profuse when he realized that the file and the check presumably had gone to dead storage in our garage, where a search would take hours or even days. The solution was a replacement check— again for 8 cents—which this time was promptly cashed.

The North Texas Building in those days not only housed most of the active trial bar of Dallas, but on the ground floor and basement levels, respectively,

it housed two remarkable Dallas institutions—Bogan's Market and Schmalzreid's book
store.

Bogan was an ingenious merchandiser. He inau-
gurated an early and successful self-service dis-
count food store. It had all of the basic economy fea-
tures which chains like A & P and Kroger have since
turned into huge and successful enterprises. And
when the Depression hit, he opened a self-service
restaurant with stand-up tables at prices so low that
it became a Mecca for any impoverished persons in
need of a good meal for little money. His staple was
a beef sandwich—a huge serving of shredded bris-
ket of beef on a bun, garnished with two dill pickle
slices—price, 5 cents. He served hundreds of
those at noon hour to people who only had 5 cents—
and to bankers and lawyers and boys like me. A
Bogan's beef sandwich and a pint of milk was a 10-
cent meal that would satisfy almost any appetite. A
remarkable mix of Dallas ate there in the thirties—
including (since he had no sit-down service) many
of Dallas's Negro citizens who couldn't eat any
place else in the downtown district. Bogan antici-
pated Harry Golden's stand-up integration plan by
two or three decades.

Sometimes, upon leaving the office for home,
Dad did the shopping for the family at Bogan's
Market. It was an interesting and occasionally agonizing process to me. Meticulously Dad recorded
the price of each item he selected. When he came to
the cashier he added up his total while the checker

was running her tape on the adding machine. Usually the machine's total and his agreed. But if they didn't, he would compare them until he found the error and insist on its being corrected. In many (perhaps most) instances, he was engaged in convincing the cashier that she hadn't charged him enough.

The Schmalzreid Book Store was located in the basement of the North Texas Building during all my youth. It fronted on Dallas's Main Street—always hot and enervating on a summer afternoon. A flight of stairs led down into the cool, quiet, and peaceful domain where Mr. Schmalzreid presided. He had no clerks and he never tried to sell a book. He cherished them all and was quite content to keep them—and acquire more to join the thousands already on his cavernous premises. He had an unwritten compact with his customers: he wouldn't bother them if they didn't bother him. He sat at a desk in the rear of the store—a wizened wisp of a man, wearing a green eyeshade and inevitably reading a book. Many times I went into the store, spent half an hour browsing, never bought a thing, and left without exchanging anything more than a wave. I think a steady customer could have read *Oliver Twist* over a period of time without ever being challenged to buy or depart.

Schmalzreid had a good selection of new books and could and would get anything that was in print. But his specialty and his pride were used books, which he bought at ridiculous prices and sold with only slight reluctance at not very much more. He had whole trays of books for 5 cents and many more trays for a dime. Incredibly, he seemed to know where in his caverns any named book was located.

Dad was one of his oldest and best customers. At times when my father found it difficult to face grocery and household bills, he bought books. He bought new books, and converted them into a library of used ones that came close to matching Schmalzreid's.

My shopping in Schmalzreid's was at the 5-cent and 10-cent tables. As can be imagined, I bought and read a host of novels that had been condemned to oblivion almost before the ink was dry.

ADVOCATE FOR
THE POOR

DAD'S PRACTICE OF LAW was trial practice. He was a poor man's advocate—by choice. most of his cases were against parties who were accustomed to winning without opposition. They rarely settled anything. Their lawyers were invariably surprised when they got the run for their money that Dad gave them. It was not entirely a labor of love for him. He tried cases brilliantly (or so I thought), and he won many of them. But the effort was exhausting, and when he won he took no great joy in the victory. His man should have won—indeed, it was an injustice that he should have been put to trial.

He had a good deal of criminal practice on behalf of a remarkably unsuccessful and penurious clientele. He represented tenants whom landlords were seeking to oust; home buyers whose homes banks were seeking to foreclose; time-payment purchasers whose stoves or refrigerators furniture houses were seeking to repossess; workmen who were being sued by (or were suing) loan sharks (Texas had a tough usury statute that was rarely enforced); and persons injured in accidents that they

believed, were a result of somebody else's negligence. In the Depression years, which I remember best, the anteroom frequently looked like the
waiting room at a big-city hospital clinic.

Dad won a case one day for one of his im-
pecunious clients. The case had involved no cash.
There had been no fee in advance, and, since the
man was unemployed, victory brought none either.
This client was distinguished only by his extreme
expressions of gratitude, which were capped by his
saying, "Mr. Edwards, I sure am sorry I can't pay
you, but I know a lot of people just like me who
need a lawyer real bad, and I'll sure bring you a lot
of business." And he did.

One case he did take a perverse sort of joy in was
that of Lizzie Henry. Lizzie's husband was old and
had become senile. He fell into the hands of a loan
shark who took a note and a deed of trust in
exchange for a loan and foreclosed on the first
missed payments. Lizzie and her husband were put
out of their house, and Lizzie came to see Dad. He
found that in addition to doing business with her
husband in his dubious mental condition, the loan
shark had also taken, recorded, and acted on his sig-
nature as a basis for conveyance of joint property.
Lizzie, it seemed, had never signed anything.

These facts being established in court in Dad's
suit to set aside the foreclosure and the deed of
trust, a decree was entered returning the property
to Lizzie and spouse. When they got back into the
house, to their joy they discovered that the loan

shark had put in running water and a bathroom—
aspects of civilization that the Henrys had never
enjoyed.

In his whole life (which certainly included some
moments of stress) I never heard my father utter an
oath. Obviously he didn't choose to, but it was also
true that he didn't need to. He had a command of
spoken English that in rare moments of anger
allowed him to employ it more effectively than any
swearing. On one occasion I heard him dress down
a woman bailiff who was known as one of the
toughest of the courthouse hangers-on. Dad believed that she had betrayed him and his client by
deliberately failing to make personal service of a
summons after he had paid her to do so. It was a
classical denunciation in clean, lean English invec-
tive, and it left her white and speechless. I judged
she had sold him out. If she hadn't been impeded
by a terribly bad conscience, she could have an-
nihilated him—she certainly had the physique and
the temper to do so.

Sometimes Dad's legal practice took on aspects
of social work. A young musician friend of his came
to him once and said he wanted to get a permit to
carry a pistol. After questioning him Dad found that
he had gotten involved with a young woman whom
he supposed to be just a woman about town, only to
learn later that she was married. He told her he was
ending their affair because he did not want to be
mixed up with a married woman. She flared up and
said, "You ain't going to drop me like that. I'll show

you. If you do I'll tell my husband and he'll get you." So Dad's friend wanted a pistol.

Dad said, "Louis, what you want is not a pistol but a railroad ticket. If that girl tells her husband and he wants to kill you, he will shoot you in the back, and you will have no more use for that pistol than if you did not have it."

So Louis bought a railroad ticket and went to Colorado. Within less than two months of Louis's departure, that same lady's husband, for exactly the same cause, went out to a construction job, and as a young carpenter climbed down a ladder, shot him in the back and killed him. Then the man and his young wife proved that that carpenter had violated the "sanctity of their home," and the murderer went free.

Juan Rivera came into the office one Saturday afternoon in February. He was a small, cold, worried Mexican American. He had a wife and seven children. He had started paying for a house several years before. He was out of a job. He hadn't made a payment in six months, and the bank had filed suit to foreclose the mortgage and repossess the house.

Dad interviewed him at some length. When he got through he said to Juan, "Well, as far as the law is concerned, you have no case at all. There's nothing wrong with the sale or the mortgage. You owe the money. You haven't paid. You can't pay. They have every legal right to foreclose, to put you out, and take the house back."

Juan said, "There's nothing we can do?"

Dad said, "Oh, I didn't say that. You may not have a legal defense, but we might think of something. Did you ever hear of the importunate widow?"

Juan said, "No."

Dad said, "Well, never mind. Your case is set for trial on the twenty-ninth. I'll file an answer and a general denial and a motion to dismiss. On the twenty-ninth you and your wife and all seven children be at the courthouse at fifteen minutes to nine. Have the children cleaned up and dressed up and bring them all, including the baby. As soon as the courtroom door is open, all of you go in and sit down on the front bench. Keep the children quiet. Don't say anything. Don't do anything. When the judge comes in, you just look at him. He's the man who has to decide whether you stay in or get out of your house. You and your wife and your children look at him as if you wanted him to leave you in your house. Who knows, maybe he'll wait until spring to sign the orders."

On the twenty-ninth Dad talked about the case at dinner. Juan and family were there early. They sat in the front row. When the judge came in and took the bench, they all looked at the judge. Dad said when he looked back all he could see were sad-looking brown eyes. The bank's lawyer put a witness on to prove the note, the deed of trust, and that no payments had been made in six months. He asked for foreclosure and repossession. Dad said he didn't really seem to have much enthusiasm about the matter.

Dad conceded the facts. He told the judge Juan had paid regularly all the time he had a job, that he wanted to pay, that he would pay just as soon as he got a job, and that it was cold weather in which to evict a man, his wife, and seven children.

The hearing didn't last long. When it was over, Dad met Juan and his family in the hall. Juan asked, "Did he put us out?"

Dad said, "No."

"He'll let us stay till spring?"

"No," said Dad, "the judge dismissed the case. He said the bank could refile its suit when its equities were stronger. Maybe the bank will appeal— but that will probably take a year."

And to us Dad added, "I think the bank may not even appeal. Their lawyer said afterward, 'I suppose if we appeal, those seven kids will be sitting in the front row in Austin, too.'"

Dad did not reject business clients, and some came to him. Frank Winn, one of my closest friends in Dallas, had an uncle who was one of Dad's business clients. The uncle's political views were about as far apart from Dad's as possible, and he was challenged on this score one day by a friend. The client's reply was simple: "George Clifton Edwards got me more money in that condemnation suit than any other lawyer I know would have."

The clearest indication, however, as to the de-

liberateness of Dad's choice in serving as an advocate for the poor of Dallas came in the midst of
the Depression. Mother, with obvious pride in her
husband's principles (mixed, perhaps, with just a
tinge of regret), told me that in our family's worst
Depression year, Dad had rejected a retainer that
was worth more than he made that whole year. It
seems that Dad had won several usury cases against
the largest small-loan company in Dallas. After the
last of these—and when Dad had no litigation pending with that company—the loan-company president came to see Dad and sought to retain him to
handle its defense of usury cases. Regrettably there
is no verbatim record of the rejection.

JURY TRIAL

THE FIRST jury trial that I ever watched from start to finish was a negligent-death case. It resulted from an automobile accident on a Sunday morning at the then rural intersection of Lemmon Avenue and Mockingbird Lane. Dad's client was the widow of a man who had been a passenger in a Ford traveling south toward Dallas on Lemmon Avenue. He and some companions were returning from a hunting trip, and he was sound asleep in the right front seat. The man was killed when, according to his surviving widow's evidence at trial, a Cadillac, driven by a man who was returning home from an early morning round of golf at the Brook Hollow Country Club, ran through the stop sign facing him at Lemmon Avenue and crashed at high speed into the middle of the Ford.

The hunter left a widow and three small children—compelling objects of sympathy. Between his survivors, his sudden and faultless death, the positive testimony by his surviving companions as to the other driver's going through the stop sign, and the defendant's involvement (however blameless) with a country club and a Cadillac, the case had many of the aspects of a negligence lawyer's dream. The case also had its problems.

My father was one of the rare lawyers in those days who employed discovery. He took the defendant's deposition and learned that the defendant was going to testify that he did stop, that he didn't hit the Ford, that, on the contrary, it hit him. And to cap the climax, he had photographs of his Cadillac showing heavy damage on his left rear—and no place else.

Dad showed me the pictures of the Cadillac that night. He was obviously concerned about the development. He had pictures of the Ford also, and they showed damage but only on the right side, directly at the right front door.

I knew that intersection. I had to cross it every time I went to Crumptown. Mockingbird Lane at that time was a gravel road. It crossed Lemmon, which was a paved road, at an angle toward Dallas. The Cadillac had to come up a small rise to the intersection. I am afraid that I accepted without question our witnesses' testimony that the Cadillac ran the stop sign at high speed. I was sure that the Cadillac driver had seen the impending collision too late, turned hard to the right, had spun, and the Cadillac's left rear had smashed into the middle of the Ford's right side.

The trouble with this theory was that nobody who was on the scene was going to testify that the accident happened that way. Our witnesses were sure the Cadillac drove straight into the middle of their car. When asked about the undamaged front end of the Cadillac, they said they did not under-

stand it. Since the plaintiff has the burden of proof,
that answer, however truthful, was hardly likely to
win a law suit. The Cadillac driver in his deposition
had stuck stubbornly to his story of stopping, pull-
ing out on Lemmon Avenue, and having the Ford
run into his rear. He couldn't explain the undamaged front end of the Ford either. But he didn't
have to. He didn't have the burden of proof.

I told Dad my theory and proposed that we go
out to that intersection in our car and try it out.
Early on the next Sunday morning, we did. Dad
stood on the left side of Mockingbird Lane in the intersection where he could see both ways and sig-
naled to me that all was clear. I took off for the intersection. Approaching it, I braked and turned, but I
braked too early and turned too late and merely
skidded to a relatively straight stop. I had skidded a
good distance on the gravel, and I was still sure we
were on the right track. The next time I approached
the intersection faster, waited a little longer, and
then turned and braked at the same time. The car
went completely out of control, spun clear around
and nearly went into the ditch on the other side of
Lemmon Avenue. It was an experience I didn't
have any ambition to repeat, even if Dad, who was
much disturbed by the spin, would have let me. But
for certain at some point in that spin the left rear of
our car had been the lead point of the automobile
mass that was traveling north through that intersection.

No doubt Dad would have found the solution to

his problem without me. He was a good enough lawyer to look for help when he had troubles. He had already made an appointment with an automobile mechanic and ex-race driver named Joe Kopecky. To my great joy, Dad told me some days later that Kopecky believed the accident had happened as I believed it had and would testify for him as an expert witness.

The case came up for trial during the summer of 1929. I had graduated from high school that June and was going to enter SMU that fall. I spent that summer, as I did most summers, at the law office, answering the phone, running errands, filing papers, reading, and carrying Dad's brief case to court.

The day before the trial began, Dad got the list of prospective jurors and spent a good deal of time identifying and making notes about each one. Dallas had a population of nearly a quarter of a million then, but the Edwards family had been there since 1871—much longer than most. If Dad didn't know anything about one of the persons on the jury list, one of his brothers was likely to. Uncle Pat was a lawyer and a cherished younger brother whom Dad had helped through law school. It seemed natural enough to me that Dad should call him and talk about several of the possible members of the jury. But he also called Uncle Will and Uncle Walker and talked quite a while to the latter.

On the day of the trial Dad awakened me early, and we left the house before Mother and Nicky were up. On such rare occasions we ate breakfast

together at Lang's Café on Main Street. By Dad's
identification of the customers, I knew that Lang's
was the early-morning gathering place for the bankers, the judges, the businessmen, the lawyers—the
great or near great of Dallas. The customers at
Lang's impressed me, but the food impressed me
more. Platters of country fried ham and eggs, pan
fried steaks with grits and by all odds my favorite—
thick, fluffy pancakes with bacon and cane syrup.

Dad and I both had pancakes and bacon that
morning, and I mentioned the calls about the jurors
of the night before. I must have said something that
implied surprise that he would have called my
uncles, because he laughed and said, "Oh, we dis-
agree on a lot of things, but we are a strong family
nonetheless. When one of us Edwardses has a
problem, it is a problem to us all. It's always been
that way."

We were in the courtroom well before nine. At
nine, while the jury panel was filing in, the clerk
came out and called Dad and the opposing lawyer
into the judge's chambers. The conference didn't
last long. The Cadillac driver had insurance, but the
insurance-company lawyer had not offered any settlement. Now with trial about to begin, they offered
(as I remember it) $5,000 or $6,000. Those were the
days when jury awards of $10,000 to $15,000 in a
death case were not unusual. But for the death of a
young man who left a widow and three small
children! Dad talked with the widow and recom-
mended that they try the case. She agreed.

The members of the jury were taking their seats as their names were called. The judge took the bench, and our case was called. The judge made a brief statement about the nature of the case, asked a few questions as to whether any of the prospective jurors knew anything about the matter, knew the parties or their lawyers, or knew any reason why they couldn't try and decide the issues fairly, and then said, "Mr. Edwards."

As the jurors' names had been called, Dad had checked them on his list. Now he arose, addressed the bench, "Your honor," and turned toward the jury panel. He called the first juror by name, asked a few questions about where the man worked and where he had gone to school. The questions themselves showed that Dad knew a good deal about him. Then he asked the juror whether he knew of any reason why he couldn't try the case fairly, as far as Dad's client was concerned. Receiving a negative answer, Dad passed on to the next juror and addressed him likewise by name. At that point I realized that he didn't have the jury list and had no notes with him.

He moved easily from one prospective juror to another, addressing each by name, asking each two or three questions, almost every one of which implied prior knowledge about the juror. "Are you still working at Sangers?" "What department are you in now?" To each one he gave a friendly invitation to tell him any reason why he might be under any influence that could be hostile to his client.

After a question or two addressed to the fifth juror, Dad said, "Now, Mr. Hill,[1] your sister Annie is still living with your family, isn't she?"

An affirmative answer brought the next question.

"And is she still working in the claims department of the Dallas Street Railroad?"

"Yes," again.

Then, "Now, from time to time she talks to you folks about the sorts of cases which come into her department, doesn't she—I don't mean names or details, but the types of problems she has to deal with."

"Well, she doesn't tell us names, but she sometimes does talk about the sort of people she sees every day and the sort of claims they make."

Dad turned to the judge and said, "Now, your honor, it is no reflection on Mr. Hill, but in view of his sister's occupation and the fact she is living in the same home, I think Mr. Hill should be excused for cause."

And Mr. Hill was excused.

Dad turned to the next juror and addressed him by name. As he got to the end of the row of jurors, there was a low buzz in the courtroom, such as there is in the stands at the end of six innings of no-hit pitching. Everyone, including me, was wondering whether Dad would go on to the second row without stopping—or, as he had every right and reason to do, simply go back to his table and consult

1. The names used in the balance of this chapter are fictitious.

his notes. There was no turning back. Dad's questions to this juror were brief and he turned directly to the first juror in the second row. Obviously, memory of Mr. Woods's name had been no problem at all.

"Now, Mr. Woods," Dad started coldly, "you know me, don't you?"

"Well, I've heard of you and probably seen you around the courthouse" was the answer.

"Now, Mr. Woods, actually you've known me since I taught at the old Central High School, haven't you?"

Woods denied such a memory.

"And you know defendant's counsel, Mr. Sanford, too, don't you?"

Woods squirmed in his chair, but replied, "Well, I've seen him around the courthouse, too."

"Have you ever done any work for Mr. Sanford or his firm?"

Woods's answer was, "Can't remember that I have."

It was obvious that Dad considered Woods to be a hostile juror and wanted to be able to challenge him for cause. It also became obvious that Woods was going to do anything he could to avoid that result—and that he was capable of being clever about it. In the end Dad suggested his disqualification to the bench because during the judge's original questioning of the jury Woods had denied knowing any of the parties or their lawyers, and now had guardedly admitted some acquaintance with both counsel. After the judge asked the juror a couple of questions about any prejudice his acquaintance might produce (Woods steadfastly denying any), he denied the motion.

Without any wasted motion or drama, Dad moved quickly through the balance of the jurors, calling each by name, asking a question or two, and then asking for any reason, if there were such, why he couldn't give the plaintiff a wholly fair trial. On the last man he was rewarded by the prospective juror reporting that his brother had been a defendant in an automobile accident case where the juror thought the brother had gotten a bad deal. He was excused.

Dad turned to the bench and told the judge that he had no more challenges for cause, whereupon the court announced a recess.

Dad had avoided any dramatics in calling each juror by name, and at recess he continued to do so. He told me that he always tried to question jurors by name and usually succeeded in doing so without notes, but he added that this panel had been easier than most, since he knew or had known about a number of the jurors. However that may be, it was a memory feat which in a lifetime in the courts I have never seen any other lawyer attempt.

Dad was mostly interested in talking about Mr. Woods. "That fellow was lying by the yard. He sells real estate and testifies in court on real-estate appraisals. I am almost certain he lied when he testified that he had not worked for Sanford's firm. But

I know he was lying about me. He was one of the most active supporters of the recall campaign against the Board of Education in 1907 and he went around town making speeches against me. I could have got him disqualified all right, but I didn't want to get that campaign involved in this trial. Well, we certainly have to use a peremptory challenge there. But I think we have a good jury aside from him."

Dad had made his memory feat sound simple, but drama plays a role in a jury trial, and this was a tough act to follow. Sanford was not without resources himself. When court reconvened and the judge called on him, he arose, greeted the jury, and said, "Now, Mr. Edwards has asked you a lot of questions, and I've got the right to ask you some more. But you look like a fine group of fair-minded people, and I am just not going to waste any of your time. Your honor, the defendant is satisfied with the jury."

Dad, of course, struck Mr. Woods's name and one or two others. And in spite of his statement of satisfaction, Sanford used most of his peremptory challenges. According to the Texas practice, the clerk struck the challenged jurors, and called the first twelve of the remaining jurors to the jury box and swore them in.

The trial was on.

What I remember best about this case is the beginning and the end. The trial itself was unexceptional. Our witnesses' testimony went into the record just about as I have related it, and Sanford's cross-examination did not seem to me to reach pay dirt. Joe Kopecky proved to be an excellent witness—knowledgeable and not easy to confuse.

I thought that the defendant made a pretty good appearance, too. On cross-examination Dad did get him to agree that he probably hadn't stopped dead. He had emphasized a bit too strongly that he had shifted into second, and Dad put Kopecky back on the stand in rebuttal to testify that you could shift into second from high in defendant's Cadillac at 40 miles per hour. Dad's closing argument had no oratorical flourishes, but he argued the negligence facts effectively and certainly made everybody in the courtroom aware of how important the loss of that life was to the widow and her three children. I was a highly partisan person to be judging, but I didn't see how Sanford could answer effectively and I didn't think he did. The judge, who seemed to me to have been calm and fair throughout the trial, gave his charge to the jury. The issue, as he stated it, really came down to whether the jury would believe that the defendant had stopped as he somewhat equivocally claimed or believe the mass of evidence to the contrary. He charged that the car in which our man had been traveling had the right of way. I didn't see how we could lose.

When the jury went out to consider its verdict, I said as much to Dad. Said he, "Son, don't ever think you can be sure about a jury trial. I think we're right. I think we ought to win. And I think most of

that jury is for us. But you never know what will
happen when you have to get twelve men to agree
unanimously. And you can never tell what they will
do with the special issues. That one I talked so
much about is the insurance companies' best
friend."

I didn't pursue the matter. I just thought he was
being cautious. And I was sure.

The jury was out for four or five hours—long
enough to set me to worrying. And then came word
that they were ready to report. The courtroom filled,
the jury filed in. The judge then asked the foreman
for the jury's answers to the special issues on which
Texas tries negligence cases.

They answered "yes" to the question about the
defendant's negligence, and "no" to the question
about the plaintiff's deceased husband's contribu-
tory negligence (a question Dad had argued vigorously should not have been submitted). They obviously were for the plaintiff all the way. When
the foreman got to the issue pertaining to plaintiff's
damages, I heard him say $35,000. I could barely
keep from cheering. That sum sounds small now,
but forty-five years ago it sounded mighty big.

Suddenly I saw Dad on his feet asking that the
jury be polled on their answer to the fifth special
issue, and each juror in turn said that he had answered it the way the foreman had reported. The
judge thanked and excused the jury and recessed
court. I saw Dad talking to the widow. He was talk-

ing very seriously and shaking his head. The courtroom was clearing, and soon he picked up his brief
case and joined me outside the rail.

I said, "Dad, that's great."

He said, "No, son, it wasn't. The jury answered
that fifth question wrong. That's the insurance-company friend that I told you about. It means a mistrial, and we have to start all over."

I protested that the jury obviously was for the
plaintiff all the way.

Dad said, "Do you remember the question, 'Do
you find that this accident was not an unavoidable
accident?' [2] The jury answered that question "no."
Technically, that means that they found that the accident was unavoidable, and you can't collect damages for a blameless accident. Sanford will move to
set aside the verdict and declare a mistrial and the
judge will have to grant the motion."

"Dad," I said, "that just can't be right."

"It certainly isn't right," he said, "but it is the
law in Texas."

This was the same summer when my father had
me start to read law. Texas still allowed admission
to the bar to those who read law for several years
under the supervision of a lawyer and then proved
able to pass the bar examination. Dad started me on
Blackstone's *Commentaries on the Common Law*. I
was supposed to read a chapter a day. In any

2. Several years after trial of this case, the Texas courts changed
this special question because of the confusion it had caused.

number of biographies of judges and lawyers, you will find tribute paid to Blackstone for the important contribution he made to their legal education. Well, Blackstone had a profound effect on my early legal education, too. He almost ended it before it began. I read him with all the comprehension I would have brought to Sanskrit. Devoted to ancient English custom and tradition, turgid of expression, and profoundly oriented toward property rights, Blackstone was the last text that was likely to excite my fifteen-year-old interest. For a man whose social thinking was continually fifty years ahead of his time, Dad had a somewhat perverse devotion to the classics.

Take just this for a sample:

The court of *arches* is a court of appeal belonging to the archbishop of Canterbury; whereof the judge is called the *dean of the arches;* because he anciently held his court in the church of Saint Mary *le bow* (*sancta Maria de arcubus*), though all the principal spiritual courts are now holden at doctors' commons. His proper jurisdiction is only over the thirteen peculiar parishes belonging to the archbishop in London; but the office of dean of the arches having been for a long time united with that of the archbishop's principal official, he now, in right of the last-mentioned office (as doth also the official principal of the archbishop of York), receives and determines appeals from the sentences of all inferior ecclesiastical courts within the province. And from him an appeal lies to the king in chancery (that is, to a court of delegates appointed under the king's great seal), by statute 25 Hen. VIII. c. 19, as supreme head of the English church, in the place of the bishop of Rome, who formerly exercised this jurisdiction; which circumstance alone will furnish the reason why the popish clergy were so anxious to separate the spiritual court from the temporal.

The court of *peculiars* is a branch of and annexed to the court of arches. It has a jurisdiction over all those parishes dispersed through the province of Canterbury in the midst of other dioceses, which are exempt from the ordinary's jurisdiction, and subject to the metropolitan only. All ecclesiastical causes, arising within these peculiar or exempt jurisdictions, are, originally, cognizable by this court; from which an appeal lay formerly to the pope, but now by the statute 25 Hen. VIII. c. 19, to the king in chancery.

Between Blackstone and that fatal special question, I rejected law for good—or at fifteen, so I thought.

A NIGHT WITH THE
KU KLUX KLAN

ONE EVENING during the spring term in my first year at Southern Methodist University, I came home to dinner with some eagerness to hear the most recent developments on the *Hurst and Coder* case. These were two young men who had greatly excited the authorities in Dallas by undertaking a series of open-air meetings in the city parks and streets. They were saying such revolutionary things as that all men were created equal and that if they only knew it, black and white workers had many things in common. It was clear to Dallas that they were dangerous men. They admitted being aliens from Kansas City. If they were communists, as the papers repeatedly alleged, they never got around to preaching their economic philosophy or their revolutionary strategy. To Dallas authorities, however, an ounce of prevention was worth a pound of cure. Hurst and Coder were promptly arrested and charged with being vagrants. All three newspapers reported the arrests in headlines.

Dad was the ACLU lawyer in Dallas, and cases like this (lots of work and no fee) came naturally to his office. The second day of Hurst's trial before a police-court judge was set for a Saturday morning, and I had attended it. The judge was a feisty man named Cavin Muse. From the very outset he had made it obvious that "Red agitators" who preached "Nigra equality" in Dallas parks would find a vigorous brand of Texas justice in his court. My father's objections to these and other judicial interpositions were summarily overruled. A jury was chosen with little or no *voir dire* examination allowed, and the trial commenced.

The testimony of the arresting officers seemed to me to be both explicit and truthful. They had seen Hurst and Coder in City Park distributing printed leaflets entitled "Black and White Workers Unite" and giving the time for a meeting at the bandstand on Sunday afternoon. The police attended the meeting, and both Hurst and Coder spoke. Both of them talked about race equality and called for blacks and whites to join unions together. The police arrested them while Coder was still speaking. The charge was vagrancy. At the police station each was found to have over $20 in his possession.

At the conclusion of the police testimony, Dad got to his feet and moved to dismiss the charges. He pointed out that under Texas law proof of possession of money for a night's lodging and meals rebutted the charge of vagrancy. Judge Muse promptly denied the motion with another speech encompassing his dislike for legal technicalities and Reds and his admiration for Texas justice and Texas juries.

Dad's cross-examination of the arresting officer was designed to answer the interesting question of exactly why he had arrested the defendants. It quickly became apparent that the officer understood vagrancy to encompass such patently illegal activities as agitating workmen and advocating racial equality.

At this point my father undertook to read various passages from the Bible that dealt with brotherhood to see whether the officer would likewise consider that reading them was illegal. The judge needed no objection from the prosecutor. He promptly ruled out any questioning of this variety and any quotation of the Bible. This ruling resulted in Dad's moving to dismiss the charges on the ground that the Texas vagrancy statute, if interpreted as forbidding these forms of speech, was patently unconstitutional under the First Amendment. The judge promptly overruled this motion also, seeming to imply that the United States Constitution was not entirely applicable to Texas.

A somewhat heated exchange followed in which my father made it exquisitely clear in polite language, that he did not think much of the judge's legal knowledge. This ended with the judge resorting to the ultimate judicial power. He found my father in contempt of court and fined him $10. Dad pulled out a $10 bill, handed it to the clerk, and said, "Very cheap for contempt of this court." The judge promptly upped the ante to $100 and a day in jail and recessed the court for lunch.

Dad stayed in the city hall under arrest until I could reach my Uncle Pat—also a lawyer—to get a writ of *habeas corpus* from the Dallas County District Court. Then we went to lunch together, picking up, upon our return, the afternoon newspaper. The headline was "Reds Lawyer Jailed."

The trial continued in much the same vein in the afternoon, except that the judge seemed a bit sobered by the *habeas corpus* writ and a bit less exuberant in his interpolations. Both Hurst and Coder wanted to testify, and did—against Dad's advice. Their stories hardly varied an iota from those told by the police. As is so often true in a jury trial, at least everybody in the courtroom knew what really happened no matter what construction was placed on the events. Hurst and Coder seemed to me to be young men who were quite sincere although not too bright. They had both acquired some of the jargon of the *Daily Worker* of the thirties, but the prosecutor didn't seem to be conscious of the slogans that might have served him best.

The judge was back in character in his charge. It was both florid and vague and gave the jury ample room to convict the defendant for what he admitted he had said. It took the jury little time to bring back a guilty verdict and even less for the judge to administer sentence and to deny Dad's motion for bond pending appeal. Hurst and Coder were taken back to jail.

All of this, of course, was reported in the Dallas newspapers over the week end and was much discussed by friend and foe alike at the *Co-op* (the SMU bookstore) and at the fraternity house the following week.

In midweek there was a strange development in the *Hurst* case. On Wednesday, March 4, the city prosecutor who had tried the case filed motions to grant a new trial and to dismiss the case. The motions, elaborately worded, read in part: "Bearing in mind that this may be our political crucifixion, and also remembering that we drink with honor to the memory of Simon of Cyrene, and remembering with pity the cowardly conduct of Pontius Pilate, we move the court to grant a new trial and dismiss the cause."

This, of course, meant that the city prosecutor's own conscience had moved him to try to correct an unjust result. It did not, however, sway the judge. Judge Muse called in Police Chief Trammel to ask whether he sympathized with the motion, and noted that he did not. Judge Muse then refused the motions summarily.

On Thursday, March 5, I found a tense atmosphere when I came home for dinner that evening. Mother had wept over the "Reds Lawyer Jailed" headline. Now she met me at the door and steered me away from Dad. In the kitchen she told me that just before he had left the office, Dad had talked by telephone with Police Chief Trammel. Trammel had indicated that the city would drop all charges, including the contempt proceedings if Hurst and Coder would leave town. He indicated that he

could get the judge's approval. On his way home,
Dad had gone by the city jail and Hurst and Coder,
who meantime had been beaten up in jail by a
prize-fighter trusty, had both agreed. Mother was in
a mood fiercely protective of her husband. She
made it clear that Dad was deeply disturbed by the
principle involved. Hurst and Coder had a right to
speak in the parks; they had a right to be in Dallas;
they had a right to believe whatever they believed,
the *Dallas Morning News*, the *Dallas Times Herald*,
the *Dallas Dispatch*, a Dallas jury, and Judge Cavin
Muse to the contrary notwithstanding. Mother had
supper ready for me and had me eat it quickly.
Hurst and Coder were to be released to Dad at 8:00
P.M. at the city jail, which was located in the basement of the Dallas city hall. I was to drive Dad to
the city hall.

On the way downtown we talked very little. I
had no feeling that my father was apprehensive, but
it was clear that he didn't like the bargain that had
been struck. I drove him to the Harwood Street entrance to the city hall. He told me to park the car in
the library parking lot just a block away and meet
him on the corner in front of the library. I saw him
walk into the basement entrance to the City Hall
where both the police department and the city jail
office were located. As I drove across Commerce
Street, I noticed three cars parked beside the city
hall on Commerce Street with a number of men
standing near them. At the time I didn't think anything about them. We were in downtown Dallas, lit-

erally within a stone's throw of the central headquarters of the Dallas Police Department.

The library parking lot was full and I had to park
on the street several blocks away. I went back to the
corner across from the city hall, noticing with some
uneasiness that the three cars and the men were
gone. I waited for quite a while. I had ample time to
recall that the three cars I had seen had had their
doors open, motors running, and wheels cut out
from the curb. Finally I went to the jail office—saw
no one—thought they must have gone out another
exit—looked with increasing apprehension at each
of the entrances, the corridors inside, and sidewalks
outside.

I knew Dad would never have left the city hall
without me and that something had happened. By
now I was remembering everything I knew about
the Ku Klux Klan. In 1931 in Texas in connection
with any unexplained episodes of violence, the
Klan came automatically to mind. In my boyhood
the Klan not only preached bigotry, it enforced its
theories on race and morality by night riding, kidnaping, tar and feathers, and the lash. There was
little or no interference from law enforcement.

My father had been a vocal opponent of the Klan
at times when voices raised against it were few indeed. For the preceding decade the Ku Klux Klan
had been the dominant fact of political life in the
state. In the early twenties it would have been hard
to find a political officeholder in Texas who wasn't a
member of the Klan.

In 1924 an avowed Klan candidate for governor
of Texas had received over 400,000 votes. It had
taken the strangest combination of farmers, la-
borers, populists, bankers, businessmen, and arch
conservatives in the history of Texas to barely stave
off that threat. The defeat had not stopped the Klan.

Not too long before I had seen the Klan march.
Dad, Mother, Nicky, and I had been swimming at
the Lake Cliff Park pool. On the way home our car
had been hopelessly caught in a traffic jam at a main
street. I worked my way through the crowd and suddenly found myself watching a Ku Klux Klan
parade. White-robed and -hooded men filled the
street in both directions as far as I could see. If there
was a fiery cross, it had gone by before we got there,
but the masked faces, the numbers, the military
cadence—and the silence—were terrifying.

But this was a civilized city. This was the city
hall. Here was the police department. This had to
be my imagination. Maybe Dad and his clients were
in an office at the jail or the police department just
across the way—waiting for me. I hurried back to
the jail office.

There were three men in the outer office—one
was a sergeant. I said, "I am looking for my father,
George Clifton Edwards."

There were mutual glances. One of the men
grinned and turned away. The sergeant said, "He
ain't here. He left some time ago."

I said, "What about the clients he was to meet?"

"They left with him."

I expect my voice was now close to breaking, but I continued, "But I was supposed to drive them to the railroad station."

Now the sergeant's voice was rougher, "Can't help it, buddy, they've left. They're gone. Maybe they took a cab." He closed a book in front of him and turned away.

The next hours were the longest I had ever known. I spent them all in the city hall or its immediate environs. I went to the police department headquarters and got even less information and no help—or sympathy. I went back to the jail office. I haunted the basement corridors. Twice I went back to the library parking lot. I was afraid to call home for fear of sending Mother into hysterics. Early in the evening I called my Uncle Pat, though I knew he was anything but enthusiastic about Dad's representing Hurst and Coder. He told me not to worry, that Dad would turn up. He tried to quiet my fears concerning the cars and the men I had seen and said the Klan wouldn't try anything like I was suggesting. He saw no need to come down to the city hall or to call the police department. I called Dad's tough-fibered older brother, Uncle Walker, only to find that he wasn't at home. I had the same luck with Dad's associate in legal practice.

On my third or fourth visit to the jail office, the same sergeant to whom I had first talked finally took pity on me. "Listen, son," he said, looking right at me, "you go on home now. Your daddy ain't going to be hurt." The way he said it I knew that he knew

exactly what he was talking about. In a sense it did
give me a sort of comfort. Lynchings were still com-
monplace episodes in the South—even though not
in Dallas County. I felt that whatever the plan was,
the sergeant knew it and that it did not involve
lynching my father. But I also felt just as certainly
that I had confirmation that he and his two clients
had been kidnaped. And no reassurances had been
tendered as to the clients at all. It may not have
been very bright of me, but I knew of nothing to do
but to stay where I was, periodically going back to
the police department and to the jail office to report
that Dad had not showed up and to ask for help to
find him.

Finally, on one of these visits one of the men in
the jail office told me there was a phone call for me.
It was Uncle Pat. He was at our house. Dad had
been kidnaped at gunpoint on the city hall steps.
He had not been hurt and was back at home. No one
knew where Hurst and Coder were. I was to come
home.

I walked the several completely deserted blocks
to where I had parked the car. Once a car passed me
cruising slowly. The four men in it stared at me and
then it turned at the next corner. I felt sure they
were coming back. As soon as they were out of
sight, I ran for the car. I started it and drove home. I
have never been so scared in my life—before or
since.

At home my mother greeted me in tears. My father was grim and shaken. When he had gotten to

the jail office at 8:00 P.M. Hurst and Coder were released to him, and they left by the same Harwood Street entrance where Dad had gone in. Three cars and six or eight men with drawn guns met them as they walked out the door. They put Dad in one car and the other two men in the other cars and quickly drove away. The whole affair was a matter of seconds, and the three cars were out of the downtown area, heading toward the countryside south of Dallas. One man held a gun on Dad. There was little conversation. At one point one of the abductors noticed that Dad had a Masonic emblem in his buttonhole and asked him what degree. Dad answered, "Thirty-second." That seemed a satisfactory enough answer. Shortly afterward the car stopped on a dark piece of country road, and they put Dad out, telling him to go home and to talk to no one about the events of the night.

He did go home. It took him some time to do so, and when he finally got a ride, he went by the library corner, hoping to find me. But he certainly did talk about the events of the night.

Dad had no hope that the police or local prosecutor would act. He decided to go to the United States attorney, the United States District Court, and the Dallas Bar Association to report the kidnaping.

Before the story broke in the newspapers as a result of those reports, on Friday, March 6, 1931, the *Dallas Dispatch*, an afternoon paper, printed a by-line account of the crime with many details about which we knew nothing. The story said that Hurst and Coder had been taken to a field in the Trinity River bottom some miles south of Dallas and had been beaten unconscious with doubled ropes. The reporter's name was Edmund Barr.

The next day the Executive Committee of the Dallas Bar Association released a resolution condemning the breakdown of law and order represented by the kidnaping and a telegram to the governor of Texas asking for an investigation of the crime by the Texas rangers. The pressure for some investigation of the kidnaping grew, and the prosecuting attorney summoned a grand jury to investigate. Barr (the *Dispatch* reporter) was subpoenaed and refused to divulge from whom he got the story. The judge in charge of the grand jury thereupon sent him to jail. After spending one day there, Barr agreed to talk and named Norman Register, a clerk in the office of the prosecuting attorney, as the man who called him on the telephone and gave him the story of the kidnaping and the beatings.

Barr was released, and Register was called before the grand jury. The *Dallas Journal* for March 12, 1931, reported that Barr met Register on the steps of the criminal court's building and conversed with him while they walked slowly across to the old courthouse where the grand jury was meeting. Before the grand jury, Register denied making the phone call or knowing anything about the kidnaping. No action was taken against him.

Meanwhile, we still had no knowledge as to the whereabouts or the fate of Hurst and Coder. Against my normal optimism, I had concluded they were dead—buried somewhere in the Trinity River bottom. We got constant rumors at the house to support my fears. Dad had had to go to Weatherford in west Texas to try a case, and the prosecuting attorney implied that his unavailability was contrived. Mother felt bad enough about the public criticism and was doubly worried about being left alone in the house with Nicky and me for the four days of Dad's case in Weatherford. Fear of the Ku Klux Klan in those days was pervasive.

Finally, on March 12, seven days after the kidnaping, Hurst and Coder arrived in Kansas City and reported their abduction to the press. The *Dallas Dispatch* story written by Barr had been correct in every essential. They had been tied to trees in the Trinity River bottom, and beaten with doubled ropes until they passed out. When they came to they made their way to a house (which they refused to identify) where a Negro family took them in, tended their wounds, and fed them for five days. On the sixth day, walking and hitchhiking, they reached Corsicana, Texas, and called Kansas City for railroad fare home.

Three weeks later Hurst came back to Dallas for the first time. Dad's laconic diary recorded the events of the two days concerned.

April 3 Drove to Fort Worth with Lewis Hurst and Andy (driving) and took a long statement from him about the kidnapping and flogging of him and Coder and home about dark. Saw U.S. Dist. Atty.

At night with O.N.E. [Dad's shorthand for Octavia

Nichols Edwards] and the children to see Ann Harding
in "East Lynn."

Grand jury whitewashed all matters.

April 4   Gave papers report on Hurst's return and
trip to Ft. Worth, which Dispatch printed.

Wrote U.S. Dist. Atty., N. A. Dodge, at Ft. Worth
about the kidnapping asking an investigation but am
rather hopeless about his doing anything. But I put it up
to him.

Dad's predictions proved accurate. No arrests
were ever made. For some time I contemplated
spending my life tracking down the perpetrators. In
time I got bravely over that thought. A couple of
years later Dad told me that he had learned the
names of eight of the mobsters. They were Klansmen. Three of them were on the prosecutor's staff.
The informant was afraid to testify for fear of his
life.

I did not then and do not now know whether
Hurst and Coder were communists. I doubt that my
father did either, although we both were aware that
they used a good deal of *Daily Worker* language in
their speeches. Dad had no use for communist
dogma. He was fiercely opposed to dictatorship of
any kind, and he thought that the advocacy or the
use of violence was wrong in principle and self-
defeating in practice. But he had not the slightest
doubt about his duty as a lawyer and a citizen to
defend with all his ability the rights of any citizen to
speak or advocate what he chose. For fifty years he
was a one-man civil liberties bureau in a jurisdic-

tion where Justice Holmes's great words from
Abrams v. *United States* were badly needed:

> But when men have realized that time has upset
> many fighting faiths, they may come to believe even
> more than they believe the very foundations of their own
> conduct that the ultimate good desired is better reached
> by free trade in ideas—that the best test of truth is the
> power of the thought to get itself accepted in the compe-
> tition of the market, and that truth is the only ground
> upon which their wishes safely can be carried out. That
> at any rate is the theory of our Constitution. It is an exper-
> iment, as all life is an experiment. Every year if not every
> day we have to wager our salvation upon some prophecy
> based upon imperfect knowledge. While that experiment
> is part of our system I think that we should be eternally
> vigilant against attempts to check the expression of
> opinions that we loathe and believe to be fraught with
> death, unless they so imminently threaten immediate in-
> terference with the lawful and pressing purposes of the
> law that an immediate check is required to save the coun-
> try.

It is interesting to note that in the March 8, 1931,
Dallas News, which detailed on its front page the
story of Dad's kidnaping, there was a parallel story
about the national homage being paid to Justice
Holmes on his ninetieth birthday.

The First Amendment has always been easier to
defend in the Supreme Court than on Main Street.

My father never ceased his public campaign
against the Klan and lived to see the demise of its
power in Dallas and in much of the South. He wore
that Masonic emblem in his lapel until he died.

SOUTHERN METHODIST UNIVERSITY

MIDSUMMER IN 1930 Dad had told me very sadly that he didn't think he could find the money to send me to Harvard. I had a Harvard scholarship but it just covered tuition. And in that Depression year the fact that there was a financial problem didn't seem strange at all. Besides, the home-town school where I would go—Southern Methodist University—didn't seem to be such a bad alternative.

SMU was known as a country-club college, but it was (and is) a big factor in the life of Texas and the Southwest. Many students from North Dallas whom I knew had gone there. My sister would be there when I entered. Not without significance to me, SMU's football team was in one of its periods of national prominence.

That summer went by more quickly than most. As soon as I registered, I got calls from several fraternities—including Kappa Sigma, which Dad had belonged to at Sewanee. I was flattered but puzzled. Sometime afterward I learned that several fraternities (Kappa Sigma among them) had been put on probation by the university for low academic averages and that a rush for grinds was a necessity. That summer I only knew that I liked the Kappa Sigma group better than the others. After discovering, to my surprise, that Dad favored my pledging, I did. Years later, again to my surprise, I learned that he particularly approved my joining *his* fraternity.

My accommodation to that fraternity and it to me were interesting processes. I intend no argument for the fraternity system. The plain fact is, however, that that group of young men meant a great deal to me in three formative years. My best friend in high school, Frank Harrison, came to SMU at mid-term and I got him to pledge Kappa Sigma. With J. P. Simpson, John Flahie, and Herschell Baker, sometimes abetted by Latham Leeds, we formed a coterie within the fraternity. What really brought us together was not so much scholarship as a great deal of curiosity and an interest in argument.

We argued endlessly about everything. We also spent a lot of time speaking in French to each other to the irritation of some of the student body, who derisively called us intellectuals. We knew better, but in our own way we did what we could to liven up the SMU scene—whether by protesting Henry Nash Smith's discharge, or by signing the Oxford Pledge, or by making life miserable for Dr. McGinniss.

Let's start with this last endeavor. McGinniss was an English professor at SMU for many years.

He was a knowledgeable English scholar and a good lecturer. He also knew he was and sometimes it showed.

By chance, three of us were in McGinniss's Shakespeare class and were exposed to his set of jokes. Some of them you could anticipate a long time before he delivered the punch line. Many of the jokes were hoary with age. Discussing this, we decided on the next such occasion simply to keep absolutely straight faces. It seemed an innocent enough response and a relatively mild curative measure.

In the very next class, the three of us were seated, as usual, in the front row, and after a windup McGinniss let go a story of legendary vintage. True to our pact, the three of us looked right at McGinniss with absolutely straight faces.

The reaction exceeded our expectations. He looked at us with obviously increasing outrage. "Out," he shouted, "out, out, out!" all the while pointing to the door. This was considerably more than we had bargained for. As we closed the door and walked sheepishly down the hall, we could still hear McGinniss shouting. It took two weeks, some skillful mediation, and at least the inferred promise to laugh at his jokes to get us back in class. Whatever his fuse point, McGinniss held no grudges against us after the event was once ended.

I took economics at SMU from one of Adam Smith's most devoted admirers. His name was Donald Scott. He was completely convinced that unrestricted and uncontrolled capitalism had created in these United States the most perfect of all possible economic worlds. In 1930 in the midst of the economic disaster of the Depression, he preached that the unemployment of millions of men and the thousands of business bankruptcies were economically healthy factors that the system required in order to depress prices, thereby bringing consumers back into the marketplace to start the cycle of business moving upward again.

He was young; he was vigorous; he had a lean face with sort of a hawk nose, and a nasal twang to his speech. He reasoned with considerable force and logic and occasional touches of humor, which made him one of the favorite lecturers on the campus. And, of course, his popularity was aided by the fact that very few of SMU's students were among the many millions of the victims of the Depression.

Scott's version of economics was about as remote from Dad's as it could possibly be. All year I wrote his examinations with haste, seeking to write (and label) first the answer that he wanted, and second, the answer that I thought was right.

Scott suffered my objections with good humor, generally managing to turn them to his own advantage in whatever classroom exchanges might develop. On one occasion he had gone far enough to suggest that any governmental soup kitchens or measures to prevent starvation through welfare grants were so hostile to the capitalist system that they should not be indulged, even if it meant that

some people starved. Attempting a *reductio ad ab-
surdum*, I asked him if it would not be less painful
and more economical if the government were to
select the people who had to die and shoot them?
"There you go again, Mr. Edwards," he said.
"Don't you realize that if you undertook measures
like that, that would bring government back into
business with its usual inefficiency, graft, and corruption."

One of the perquisites of student life at SMU
was ushering at the musical events of the Fair Park
Auditorium. The management used as ushers all of
us who showed up in tuxedo an hour early. For pay
we got to take any unoccupied seats for the concert.
Some of us heard most of the concerts this way.

Once on a cold, rainy winter night, Lauritz
Melchior, the great tenor of the Metropolitan
Opera, came to Dallas. The Fair Park auditorium
seated 3,500. That night there weren't more than
250 people present. Melchior came out to the center
of the stage, sang his opening number, and then
looked out. He walked up to the footlights, and
called the 250 people who were scattered all over
the large auditorium down to the front, saying,

My friends, we have an intimate group here tonight
and we're going to have a great evening. Come down and
share it with me.

All 250 in the audience went down to the front
seats, and Melchior sang as I have never heard a
concert performer sing before or since. When he

finished the prearranged program, he asked the audience to call out numbers that they would like him to sing, and he sang on and on for that tiny audience. It was one of the greatest musical evenings of my life. More than that, it was one of the great examples of human will and genius turning an occasion that was at least a minor disaster into a magnificent event.

The best teacher I ever had (in the classroom) was Henry Nash Smith. A desire to write was a direct part of my family heritage. My father's journals are full of lectures to himself about not writing enough. He never really felt possessed of an idea until he had put it down on paper. From boyhood on I, too, was fascinated by the written word. Henry Smith and SMU added to that fascination. At the time, no one involved had any idea that my desire to write would be fulfilled principally by an almost endless series of appellate-court opinions.

Smith had graduated from Southern Methodist University and Harvard. Later he taught at Texas and Minnesota, wrote extensively on southwestern literature and culture, and became biographer of and the living authority on Samuel Clemens. He is now professor of English at the University of California at Berkeley.

When I had him for freshman English, he was young, vigorous, crew-cut, and blond. He did not indulge in classroom oratory. But for each hour he quite obviously had a plan. He pursued it in clear English diction, which was an example all in itself.

Over and above that, this calm, self-confident young
man had an intensity about him that commanded attention and respect. He made us work. We wrote
something—story, essay, or poem—every week,
and he graded them, commented on them, and returned them promptly every week.

At the end of my second year at SMU, Henry
Nash Smith was abruptly fired from the faculty for
writing an introduction to a book, *Miss Zilphia
Gant*—one of the minor novels of William Faulkner. The introduction was not exactly a paean of
praise for *Miss Zilphia Gant* or William Faulkner.
Smith was not given to extraordinary display of
emotion. He did give a detached and critical analysis of the book, and he clearly asserted that William
Faulkner was one of the most important figures
writing in America in the 1930s.

This latter was too much for Dr. John O. Beaty,
the head of SMU's English department. He considered Faulkner's works obscene and was not inclined to tolerate a difference of opinion on the
topic. Beaty was a rather handsome man who was
himself a teacher of ability. But the contrasts with
Smith were sharp. Beaty ran to fat. He was a clas-
sicist. He was a prude, and on occasion he had been
known to speak well of Adolf Hitler.

While I had been interested in various of my father's causes, Henry Smith's discharge became the
first of mine. Dad was just as outraged by Smith's
discharge as I was, but I was much closer to the
scene. I find it hard to remember now very much

that we did about it. Some of us prepared a petition asking that Smith be rehired, and we talked a lot about it—almost exclusively to people who were wholly in agreement with us and had little if any influence with the administration of SMU.

Fortunately, a lot of work on the problem was done by persons with experience, know-how, and influence, like the redoubtable McGinniss, Lon Tinkle, Herbert Gambrell, Jerry Bywaters, and Jack Hyman. Six months later Smith was rehired. The method by which the irreconcilable conflict with Beaty was resolved was interesting. Smith was made a professor in the department of comparative literature. Some years later he was quietly reassigned to the English department.

In the spring of 1932 Japan invaded Manchuria. Henry Stimson, then secretary of state of the United States, not only condemned the aggression, but threatened American intervention. The intervention suggestion ran into a storm of public protest.

At SMU, on the heels of the Stimson statement, some of us drafted and circulated an American version of the Oxford Pledge. This was a pledge originated by some Oxford students in the thirties "not to fight for King and country." We altered it to pledge not to fight in any war in which the United States might engage.

I have never been a pacifist. I have always known there were circumstances that would make me fight. But on the campus of Southern Methodist University in 1932 we could not think of such cir-

cumstances happening. The immensity of the
world, the broadness of our oceans, the peace-
fulness of our immediate neighbors—we argued all
these things as we circulated the declaration that
we would not fight.

The petition was signed by most of my fraternity, most of the leaders of student government, and
a lot of the leadership, scholastic and otherwise, of
the university. The story of the SMU Oxford Pledge
appeared in the Dallas papers, and then the storm
broke. The veterans organizations of Dallas denounced us; a counterpetition was organized; there
were statements and counterstatements. The whole
affair ended with a somewhat condescending editorial in that oracle of public opinion, the *Dallas
Morning News*, praising our antiwar sentiments, but
concluding that if the United States were ever really threatened, it had no doubt that we would
respond to the colors.

Just over a decade later Hitler had overrun
Europe, Japan had sunk the United States fleet at
Pearl Harbor and had largely overrun the Pacific.
Long before the Nazi-Japanese war machine
reached the height of its power, my antifascist con-
victions had conquered my antimilitarism.

But I still got a shock when in World War II I
found myself in an infantry training camp at Macon,
Georgia, watching an Army training film entitled
Why We Fight. It began with the Japanese invasion
of Manchuria.

I spent the last year and a half at SMU in a state

of euphoria. Today such a state suggests drugs or alcohol. My intoxicant was love.

Girls were one of SMU's major products. They were onmipresent, and institutions were built around them. Fraternity and sorority week-end dances were major events. And I participated with fair frequency. By trial and error I learned to dance a little. Occasionally I took a girl to a dance or to the ladies luncheons at the fraternity house. All of this was routine enough until I fell hopelessly in love.

The girl lived in Dallas. In her freshman year she had been chosen one of the campus beauty queens. That description, however, is hardly fair. Most campus beauty queens specialized in looks, charm, and vacuity. She was beautiful; she was charming; but she certainly wasn't dumb. She was bright, alert, and interested in a lot of things—the theater among them. She was in demand to play ingénue roles in campus and city amateur theater. She fitted easily enough into the role of the innocent and beautiful young female.

June entered SMU a year after I did. We met in McGinniss's Shakespeare class. McGinniss, if not Shakespeare, always provided conversational material for the walk to the campus store and the inevitable Cokes. Coke dates turned into fraternity-house lunch dates and then into evening dates. By the second or third of these, I knew that I was in love. I also knew that this romance had no future at all.

There were practical problems, all sorts of them. At SMU popular girls like June took pride in having

a date every night. My first problem was getting on
June's calendar at all. And my next was how to finance the dates I did secure. A date a week was
about as much attention as I could command, and it
was a good deal more than I could pay for.

There were no jobs in 1932. I couldn't see asking the family to raise my quite spartan allowance
for what I was sure would be considered frivolity.
As a result I learned to play poker—in dead earnest.

Like most boys in Texas in those days, I had
learned the rudiments of poker long ago. There was
a poker game in the attic room of the fraternity
house nearly every afternoon. I had played occasionally for fun. I had won a little and lost a little.
Now it was different. I wanted to know everything
there was to know about the game. I read books
about poker. I studied the suggestions they contained and compared them to the game that I played
in. I adopted a theory. Get a reputation as a plunger
who will bet on anything, but get it cheaply. Then
actually play the most conservative game possible
until you are sure or as reasonably sure as can be
that you have the top hand. Then bet the limit.

The game was 5 cents ante and pot limit. If I
could make myself throw in the below average
hands where otherwise I started behind, I could
save a lot of money. I decided to throw in all draw
poker hands where I had a small pair or less since
the opener had to have a pair of jacks or better.
Religiously I turned down stud hands where my
hole card was below eight. Since few at the table

had similarly compelling motivations, many played most hands through the last card. There were even some players who played every hand!

Even within my rules, there was plenty of chance to bluff—and I did, enough to see that when I had a real hand, I got calls. This was a small game. There were some good players. I held many second-best hands. Winning by my formula took time. But I never had to cancel a date.

Part of June's charm was that she was a good and sympathetic listener. From me she must have heard dreams and aspirations like nothing she had heard before. Ambition to work with the unemployed, the poor, the blacks, the peace movement—such ideas were most unlikely dinner-table conversation at her house.

We did share one aim. Both of us wanted to see much more of the world than Dallas. June talked of the theater, but obviously she wasn't going to throw her life at it. One evening she spelled out what she really expected to happen to her—marriage a year or so after SMU, three or four children, a husband who (like her own father) supplied $500 a month to run the house and pay the children's expenses and hers. It didn't sound avaricious. It was frank and, to me, it seemed a little wistful. It was all too apparent that after SMU my way was not going to be June's way, or June's way mine.

I had no hope for my first romance from the beginning, but tenuous as it was, I also had no desire to end it. June was more practical. Two weeks before graduation she told me she was not going to see me again and was going to go steady with the young scion of a Dallas chain-drug-store magnate. He had been the leading contender for that honor all the while.

Some how, without doing or saying anything that would seem to warrant the conclusion, June made me feel that I was really important to her. That feeling and the confidence it engendered remained with me. Years later I met and fell in love again with a beautiful, vital, apparently unobtainable, definitely more adventurous girl. Persistence of my pursuit of my beloved Peggy, who has now shared my life for thirty-five years, owed a good deal to that brief romance of 1932.

The closest to a real argument I ever had with my father came as a direct result of that romance. It occurred my last week at SMU. On Monday morning Dad told me he wanted to see me at the office at three o'clock that afternoon. He gave me no hint as to what the topic was, and since this had never happened before I was puzzled. By chance I had a completely uncluttered conscience. I had taken my last exam. I knew that the year's record was likely to be reasonably acceptable—even by his standards. I was committed with some enthusiasm to a graduate year at Harvard, which I knew that Dad had planned for a long time. In my mind June, SMU, Dallas (at least for a time) were over. What was there to talk about?

I got there at three o'clock. Dad took me into the

office, closed the door, sat down at his desk, pulled out a yellow legal pad, picked up his pen, and said, "Now, son, what debts have you?"

I laughed and replied that I didn't have any.

"No," he said, "I'm serious. To whom do you owe money?"

I protested that I didn't owe anybody any money except the past week's lunch bill at the fraternity house.

"Well, son," he said, "I know you have been dating and I know you have been playing poker and you haven't been getting money for either from me."

I answered, "Dad, I don't lose at poker. I win."

"Oh, I see," he said. "Well, that is bad." There was a long pause. "Well, I would like you to promise me never to play poker again—to win." I protested that that was what poker was all about. And he answered that playing poker for fun might be all right, but he didn't want me doing it to make money.

He had caught me at the wrong time. I knew that my need to win at poker was over. I felt that Dad's real concern was not poker, but June. June was gone, and I was fully engaged with my misery. But Dad had not mentioned her and I knew that he wouldn't. I didn't intend to either. And I was certainly not going to admit any evil in the method I had used to finance that brief romance. The fraternity poker game was, I asserted, a fair game among equals. Probably everybody who played in it was better equipped for the risk than I. To all of which Dad pointed out that if I won consistently, as I apparently had, I must have some advantage, and he didn't want to see me make money that way. He just didn't seem interested in the merits of not drawing to shorts or not staying at stud on hole cards less than eights.

I can't recall that he ever asked me for a commitment on anything else, but the best he got out of that afternoon was a promise to think about it. I guess I thought about it all right.

HARVARD, 1933-34

MY GRADUATE YEAR at Harvard was distinctly Dad's idea. He had gone to Harvard for an M.A. in English in 1899. William James, George Santayana, George Pierce Baker, and George Lyman Kittredge were then among the great figures at the university. The year had left a profound impression on him. I think he had planned on my going to Harvard from the day I was born.

In Dad's papers were two thick folders captioned "My Blighted Dreams of Harvard." The dreams were my father's, but they pertained to me. There was the whole story of the planning, scheming, scrimping, and saving to send me to Harvard directly from high school—a plan that, perhaps fortunately, the Depression scuttled.

Dad's alternative plan was for me to finish SMU in three years and take the fourth year of college as a graduate year at Harvard. This happened, although the plan was very nearly aborted before I ever got to Cambridge, Massachusetts.

I left Dallas in early September, 1933, with a standard Royal typewriter in one hand and a heavy old valise in the other. Quite a bit of the weight in the valise was represented by a collection of books I thought I might need. That proved to be coals to

Newcastle, but the old Royal was worth its weight.
A Greyhound bus took me and my burdens straight
through to New York City. I stopped there to see my
sister, Nicky, off to France for a year at the Sor-
bonne, where she had won a scholarship.

That week end in New York City was full of fascinating experiences and impressions. Like any
tourist, I walked across the Brooklyn Bridge and
took a ride on the Staten Island ferry. But I also
wandered through the garment district and the
tenement district on the Lower East Side, heard a
fierce street-corner debate between a Stalinite and a
Lovestonite in Union Square, and met Norman
Thomas.

Dad had given me a letter of introduction to
Thomas, who was the national chairman of the
League for Industrial Democracy. I received a
warm welcome. Thomas introduced me to Mary
Fox, Joe Lash, and Monroe Sweetland, all active
leaders of the LID. That afternoon, in the company
of Joe and Monroe, I heard Thomas speak at an
open-air meeting off Fourteenth Street. Aside from
Thomas's eloquence, the primary thing I remember
about that meeting was the vigorous heckling of an
organized cadre of young communists who tried
vigorously and unsuccessfully to break up the meeting.

Sunday evening found me at the old Greyhound
station on Forty-second Street standing in line to
buy a ticket for the midnight bus to Boston. I had
left Dallas with $400 in cash, which Dad figured

would serve to pay my tuition, board, room, and all other expenses through the first half of my Harvard year. I was impressed with the sum, but perhaps not sufficiently to keep someone near the ticket window from seeing that I had it.

As I left the station and turned toward Fifth Avenue on Forty-second Street, a well-dressed man in his thirties approached me from the opposite direction. He asked me for a direction to Fifth Avenue. That being about the only direction I was capable of giving in New York City, I was eager to point out that he was headed away from rather than toward Fifth Avenue and that I was going that way myself. By the time we reached Fifth Avenue we were fast friends. I knew all about him. By some strange coincidence he was going to Boston on the same bus that I was taking. He was a successful young advertising man in New York on business that included, among other things, selling skywriting promotions. He had an explanation, which seemed plausible at the time, as to why only the midnight bus to Boston would do for his business purposes.

At the corner of Fifth Avenue and Forty-second Street we saw an elderly gentleman in a tweed jacket, obviously tipsy, who was approaching passers-by as if to strike up a conversation. Each time he was rebuffed. We weren't surprised when he approached us, and we listened as he poured out his story excitedly and in a very British accent. He was in New York to settle the estate of a wealthy aunt who died here the preceding year. He had received

the proceeds, $12,000 in cash, this same morning,
and in celebrating his good fortune, had fallen in
with a young lady who proposed another form of en-
tertainment than liquor, of which he obviously had
imbibed quite a bit. At the hotel room she had
demanded $5, "a pound" in his parlance, but he had
only had a £2 note, whereupon she offered to go get
change while he relaxed. She never reappeared and
he vehemently wanted to get "a Bobby to put her to
rights."

My knowledgeable skywriting friend, with
much laughter, assured him that that was the last
thing he wanted to do and that in fact what he
should have done was to tell the young lady, "I'll
match you, double or nothing."

"Match, match," said the Englishman, "what's
that?" Whereupon my friend said to me, "Here,
George, let's show him," and we matched coins.
The Englishman immediately wanted to join the
game, and my friend was more than willing. "Three
can play at this game, odd man wins," he said. And
then aside to me, "This Englishman is dead drunk.
He's got a lot of money; you hold heads, I'll hold
tails, and we'll split later after dinner."

Whatever self-defense mechanisms should have
been sounding alarm were completely silent. Nor
was there any conscious recollection of Dad's recent warning against "gambling—to win." What
saved me and Dad's painfully accumulated $400
was the family underdog tradition. The helpless
Englishman stumbling over his words, lurching
about the street, dropping large bills on the pave-

ment, and then stooping down to gather them up seemed as vulnerable as a big puppy. I told my friend that I didn't want to do it. He insisted that this was a "once in a lifetime chance." That didn't make the proposal any more attractive to me. When he finally proposed that we drop into a poolroom and shoot a few games of pool, and the Englishman happily agreed, I told him I would see him on the bus, and broke away amid continued protestations.

When the midnight bus left for Boston, I was aboard it; but there was no sign of my skywriting friend. Three weeks later a Boston paper carried an article about a man who lost his life savings of $5,000 to a couple of confidence men in the Kansas City railroad station. The story said the men had posed as a skywriting salesman and a drunken Englishman.

I got to Boston at around 6:00 A.M., and by 7:15 I exited from the subway in Harvard Square, valise in one hand, typewriter in the other, rumpled, unshaven, hungry, and fogbound from another night on a bus. The first person I saw was John Lee Brooks, a fraternity brother from SMU now studying for an English Ph.D. at Harvard. He was bright-eyed, tweed-jacketed, flannel-trousered, and brisk of pace. Obviously he had slept and breakfasted well. He was smoking an after-breakfast pipe, and under his arm he had an old leather-bound volume that reeked of early English literature.

John Lee had never looked like that before. I knew I was at Harvard.

Two of the courses I took at Harvard were ones

that Dad had taken thirty-four years earlier. George Lyman Kittredge, who taught Dad Shakespeare in 1899, also taught me Shakespeare in 1933. The other course was English drama. A great Harvard professor, George Pierce Baker, had taught Dad in 1891. He apparently left an indelible imprint on this course that lasted long after he had deserted Harvard for Yale.

I saw and heard Kittredge perform by dint of auditing his Shakespeare course. Kittredge was a famous figure at Harvard then. He should, indeed, have taught drama. He had the flair. One of the sights of Harvard in the thirties was that of Kittredge crossing Harvard Square. He did not do it like any ordinary mortal, but approached the square at full stride, his shock of white hair and his magnificent beard tossed by the wind. When he reached the curb of that busy intersection, without breaking his stride (and without any regard for traffic) he flung his cane straight up in the air and charged across. This tactic produced squeals of cars and trucks being braked to a sudden stop. Occasionally an irate motorist would let out a string of Anglo-Saxon at him. Kittredge never looked to the right or left or showed the slightest concern. It was a magnificent performance. It ran for many years—and Kittredge died in bed.

I found his classroom show interesting also, but not quite up to the billing. Kittredge played to a large house. No one ever seemed to know or care who was present. But as a lecturer he was erudite, articulate, and witty. He held his audience easily and kept them coming back. He only dealt with two plays in a whole year.

Dad noted in his diary from Harvard that Kittredge could lecture an hour on a single word. Thirty-four years later he was still doing it. I felt that I was hearing much more Kittredge than Shakespeare. His lecture technique was to discuss the play line by line. Frequently his learning about Elizabethan England provided insight into the meaning of the words Shakespeare employed that was quite different from their twentieth-century meaning. But just as frequently he took a word or a sentence and suggested that it contained an allusion so remote in English or European history that I found it impossible to attribute it to Shakespeare. Some of his theories were as complicated as a murder-mystery plot, and, like them, led to only one possible solution.

I think I would have had nothing but admiration for Kittredge's pyrotechniques if he had been willing to leave a little room for doubt about his hypotheses. Kittredge, however, proclaimed his version of Shakespeare with all the certainty of a fundamentalist preacher propounding the Old Testament or a communist of the thirties demonstrating how Marx had foretold some strange twist of the Moscow line.

To me Kittredge was one of the first of many examples of Harvard's strange mixture of excellence and arrogance.

In contrast to other courses, class experience in modern English drama had no effect at all on me. As noted above, the course had been made famous by George Pierce Baker, who had taught it at Harvard for many years before going to Yale. I had taken modern English drama at SMU from a well-thought-of-professor. I knew my SMU professor had taken Baker's course at Harvard. I knew, of course, that I was bound to find some duplication when I took the same course at Harvard. But between schedule problems and degree requirements, there seemed to be no choice.

I didn't think it particularly strange that the plays we were to study were identical with those we had studied at SMU. As the lectures started, I wasn't too surprised to find some comments on the play under discussion that paralleled what I had heard before. But I was startled to hear the same jokes told about precisely the same lines of the same play.

Inquiry produced the information that my Harvard professor (like the one at SMU) had taken modern English drama from Baker. After the third lecture, I wrote home for my SMU notes and never took another note in class. What a tribute to Baker!

To tell the truth, however, that class was far from a waste. It was a big class—perhaps two hundred students. Each of us was assigned to a specific tutor. Mine was a tough-minded, knowledgeable young man whose job it was to see that I produced a thesis on a topic related to the course. Brashly I chose to write on George Bernard Shaw's political views.

Shaw had a lot of them, spread throughout his plays
and nondramatic works. I had never before under-
taken a research or writing project of such magni-
tude.

I am sure that my thesis did not contribute anything to the sum total of knowledge of anybody
other than me. It did, however, produce the only bit
of outright praise I ever remember from my father.

One of Dad's favorite stories was about an elderly lawyer in Dallas whom he quoted as saying,
"I hate flattery. I hate all flattery unless it is fulsome." Dad was warm and loving to his children
and was always sympathetic and helpful to us in
times of trouble. But he was uncomfortable in attempting praise. Although I knew he would be
pleased with the Shaw thesis, he never mentioned
it to my face. I had sent the thesis home, and I found
it years later with what he thought of it written on
the title page. It was fulsome.

One of Dad's favorite stories repeated frequently in my youth concerned a Harvard professor with a lisp. In his greeting to each class he invariably urged his students to go to the library every
day and "wead and wead and wead" and "bwose
and bwose and bwose."

Dad's enthusiasm for scholarship had matured at
Harvard. All his life it characterized his reading, his
writing, and his approach to the law. He had attempted during all my youth to convey that enthusiasm to me—without much result. At Harvard, the
seeds bore some fruit.

The pillared portico of Widener Library domi-

nates the Harvard yard. Widener also dominated
Harvard's scholastic life as I knew it. Perhaps it still
does. It is one of a dozen great libraries of the world.
In the accessibility of its information I have never
met its equal. In its stacks I first found the excite-
ment and enrichment of research.

Also on its steps on a not-to-be-forgotten day, I
met the Harvard student body face to face. I doubt
that that experience enriched any party to the encounter.

Like all graduate students in the thirties, I was
assigned a carrel in the Widener stacks. This meant
a narrow work space with book shelves and a desk,
and the freedom to range the library, to select
books, and keep them for a reasonable period of
use. I spent most of my nonclassroom hours in
Widener. All of my classes took great amounts of
reading and quite a bit of research. The thesis on
George Bernard Shaw and an advanced English
composition class took great amounts of writing.

Some skeptic defined research as learning more
and more about less and less, until finally you know
everything about nothing. Indeed, for research to
be meaningful it must have a very limited objective.
Take a single episode related in English literature
or a single historical event, go back to original and
contemporaneously written documents and frequently you discover major variances between
the views now accepted and what actually took
place. In the process you may come to believe that
as to this one matter concerning this one point in

history, you know more than anyone else in the world.

I found that research can be as exciting as a mystery novel. It surely wasn't designed that way (at least by me) but it proved to be great training for appellate opinion writing.

The Farnsworth Room was a comfortable, well-appointed reading room near the entrance to Widener Library. It had a rack of the great daily papers, and its shelves were filled with English classics. I spent an hour or so a day there reading for enjoyment. I would read as much as I could take of the news accounts of the events that were to lead ultimately to World War II and then, for surcease, turn to Galsworthy's novels and the secure nineteenth-century world where Britain still ruled the waves.

The Farnsworth Room meant more to me, however, than just a place of relaxation. There I read and thought about the inroads of fascism—first in Germany and then in Austria. Hitler had come to power in Germany in January, 1933. That same year Dollfuss's troops crushed the workers' movement in Austria and established a dictatorship. The destruction of the democratic forces in each of these countries and the increasingly menacing Nazi military threat forced me to begin rethinking my essentially isolationist position concerning my country's relations with the world.

There, too, I read Aldous Huxley's *Brave New World*. I didn't like or accept its elitism or its argument against equality. But Huxley's picture of the drab sameness of life under dictatorship and his warning about the state's power of thought control impressed me. In time I came to think that the infinite variety of America was another and important way of talking about freedom. The seeds of my adult lifetime belief in internationalism and a pluralistic society were planted in the Farnsworth Room. As will be obvious from what follows, however, I am getting ahead of my story.

Widener Library has another and quite different place in my memory. From the balustrade beside its wide steps I made an antiwar speech to some two thousand Harvard students.

I had joined the Harvard Liberal Club when I first got to Cambridge. The Liberal Club had had an illustrious history, but in recent years it had been a rather mild discussion group. By midyear some of us secured its affiliation with the Student League for Industrial Democracy. I was elected an officer of the Liberal Club, and in the spring the club sponsored the Student Strike against War at Harvard. The strike was called for 11:00 A.M. on April 13, 1934, by the Student League for Industrial Democracy and the National Student League. Antiwar demonstrations were observed on perhaps a hundred campuses by as many as 25,000 students. It was the first student strike against war in this country.

At Harvard the "strike" was quite an event, although hardly an unqualified success. It had been the subject of quite a bit of publicity in the Boston papers and in the Harvard *Crimson* beforehand. The *Crimson* in particular had ridiculed the idea, and we had reason to expect some trouble. The trouble we feared most, however, was that the event would not be noticed at all. Harvard might just go on its placid way without a glance at the steps of Widener to which we had sought to summon the student body.

On April 13 by 11:00 A.M. we knew that fear was ill-founded. We certainly hadn't been ignored. Most of the student body was on or near the Widener steps. All of our peace forces were there, apprehensive but determined. So, too, were a great many more students who had come out of curiosity. And in addition there was a corps of organized anti-demonstrators. One wore a Boy Scout uniform and carried a sign proclaiming himself the Michael Mullins Chowder and Marching Society. He carried a bugle upon which at intervals he would blow a discordant blast. Still another had dressed himself as Adolf Hitler and periodically would yell, "Sieg Heil!" and give the Hitler salute. The onlookers tended to be delighted by these antics.

The first speaker had heavy weather. He had a prepared speech and attempted to give it without deviation. To meet the bugle calls and the *Heil Hitler*s, he simply increased the decibles. There wasn't anything wrong with this except that it didn't work. After some time he gave up in frustration.

It was my turn next. I had prepared what I considered a thoughtful statement for a meeting on the

steps of Widener Library. Midway in my predeces-
sor's speech I decided to throw it away. This was
much more like the courthouse lawn or street-
corner meetings that I had frequently attended (and
occasionally spoken at) in Texas. There, if a speaker
ever let a heckler get the upper hand, he was lost.
Apparently this was also true at Harvard.

At the outset I greeted "Harvard men" (the lis-
teners) and "Harvard children" (the hecklers). The
counteroffensive drew cheers from the antiwar
forces and seemed to bother the hecklers. They
were back at it in short order, however, with bugle
blasts and shouted comments. To each of these I
made some response. The man on the podium in
this kind of exchange has an enormous advantage,
and I made full use of it. The dialogue hardly fitted
the academic setting in which it took place. Eventually "Hitler" and "Michael Mullins" left me pretty
much alone, and from memory I resurrected a good
deal of what I had originally intended to say. At the
conclusion, lunch hour at the houses was at hand.
Our chairman adjourned the meeting and "Michael
Mullins" organized a noisy parade toward the din-
ing rooms.

The news accounts of the day's events high-
lighted the activities of the oppositionists. The accounts were, however, relatively kind to me, and I
gained a brief fame (or notoriety) from that half hour
on Widener's balustrade that a solid year of reading
and writing in my carrel in its stacks would never
have occasioned.

From Dallas came a telegram, "Toujours l'audace," signed GCE.

My professors knew me after that meeting. The class I had cut to attend the meeting had been F. O. Mathiesson's modern English poetry. Mathiesson at the previous class had talked about the impending strike and had concluded that he would hold the class but that those who wished were free to cut it.

At the class after the strike Mathiesson asked me to stay for a moment. To my embarrassment he began a profound apology for not having called the April 13 class off altogether.

Mathiesson was one of the most intelligent men as well as the most melancholy and ill-starred man I have ever known.

His lectures in modern English poetry were great learning experiences. No one whom I have heard read poetry ever approached his capacity to orchestrate it. He had a beautiful voice, with depth and range. He not only knew the poems, he lived them—and he made us live them, too.

He was also tortured by an active social conscience and by the dismal parade of world and national events. Ultimately his depression became so great during the McCarthy era that he committed suicide. It was a waste of a great talent.

Human ingenuity occasionally produces triumphs of prior planning. The architect of old Emerson Hall helped produce a fascinating Harvard memory.

On a clear winter day, the sun during our ten

o'clock philosophy class struck down through the high windowpanes like a shaft of light on the raised podium of our classroom on the ground floor of Emerson Hall. Its rays created an almost mystical aura around the cherubic face, bald head, and halo of white hair of the professor.

Alfred North Whitehead in stature and visage looked a bit like Winston Churchill. His diction and eloquence were also reminiscent of Churchill. A philosophy lecture by Whitehead was more a religious experience than a normal educational exercise. Whitehead came, greeted us warmly, and then proceeded to think out loud for fifty minutes. Speaking to us, Whitehead's face often seemed to mirror the ecstasy of a vision he was seeking to share. He thought and talked about what interested him at the time—always at the edges of his knowledge and usually well beyond ours.

Whitehead played the role of genius in residence to us. He was a man with courage to adventure in ideas, to explore the unknown. The questions he raised in our minds we explored and argued about on the fourth floor of Perkins Hall until all hours.

English 15 was an advanced composition course for graduate students and a sprinkling of seniors. It was a famous course at Harvard. Famous men had taught it. And some men who had taken it had gone on to fame.

All of us who applied for it had dreams of writing for a living. Only fifteen were accepted. I was accepted on the basis of a rather gory short story. It was a fictionalized version of the fate of a young man who had been beaten to death in the Fort Worth, Texas, jail that same year.

The happy fifteen who were chosen felt that we had a guarantee that we would find the writer's Valhalla of our predecessors. We approached the class full of good will, particularly to our fellow classmates—and soon found ourselves locked in internecine combat.

A gentle poet and a minor novelist named Robert Hillyer taught the class. Perhaps mediated would be a better word. His technique was the simplest possible. The class met once a week. And each week every student had to turn in a piece of original writing—short story, essay, or poem. Hillyer would choose several such pieces for each succeeding class. He would read the piece, and then invite class comment. At first the comment was tentative and relatively sympathetic. Since all oxen were in the same boat, why start goring?

But the issues of the times were great ones. The country was in the depths of the Depression; unemployment was at the peak; the news was full of bankruptcies, suicides, starvation, and riots. Hitler was in full power in Germany; his American admirers were making shrill imitations of him here. In such a world some of us thought Joyce, Proust, T. S. Eliot were effete. When some of our classmates attempted imitations of them, we who classified ourselves as realists descended upon them with vigor.

And when a piece was read that we felt dealt with the issues of our times, it received scornful ridicule from the art-for-art's-sake group.

The difference in approach was mirrored in two first lines: "We were marching, starving, down the street" and "I was dancing naked in the moonlight." I find that I want to deny that I authored the first of these two improbabilities, but my memory insists that C. L. Sulzberger did author the second.

Sulzburger and I became spokesmen for the two opposing trends in the class. In terms of class support, I was aided by the fact that he was a Harvard senior while most of the class consisted of graduate students from other colleges. Of course, the fact that Sulzburger had been admitted at all as an undergraduate bespoke both scholarship and brilliance. But truth to tell, these qualities did not endear him to us very much either.

The schism between graduate school and college (real, I think, for all of us) was probably epitomized by my reaction. I came from a 1,200-student-body college in the Southwest. I could call almost all of the students by name. And no one—stranger or not—walked across the SMU campus without being spoken to by everyone who passed him.

At Harvard the opposite was true. No one spoke to anybody unless they had been formally introduced. And this was true even though the two passing each other had been in the same class for a year. A few attempts to change this dubious tradition had produced such cold stares as to make us non-Harvardians into believers. We, too, ceased speaking.

Sulzburger and I debated style and content of written English every week for a year in a class of fifteen. But we had never "met" each other and, hence, never spoke—even when by chance we were seated opposite each other at the Georgian across a 24-inch square table.

Years later Sulzburger was a UPI correspondent at the settlement of the first General Motors strike. I was there as a representative of the UAW. Frank Winn, then publicity director for the UAW, introduced us, saying we must have been at Harvard together. We both elected to pick up the conversation from there, without a reference to past history.

I left Harvard the first week of June, 1934. Pleasant, stimulating, good as the year had been, I had come to think of Harvard as the epitome of the ivory tower. I was eager to leave—much too eager to wait for graduation still a week away. I left much as I had arrived, walking from Perkins Hall to the subway in Harvard Square, carrying the old valise (with its unneeded books) in one hand and the Royal typewriter in the other. At one point, crossing the yard, I set my baggage down to take a last look around at the magnificent elms of the yard and at Emerson Hall and Widener Library, the buildings that meant the most to me. I was headed for the midnight Greyhound bus to New York City.

I was nineteen. I had two college degrees. I had

neither a trade nor a profession. I did have a job
at $10 a week as a college secretary for Norman
Thomas's League for Industrial Democracy. I also
knew where I would sleep that night. What more in
an insecure world did one need?

I also had a few small ambitions. I wanted to
help (1) end war; (2) end poverty; (3) end race injustice. In my spare time I thought I might try writing
the great American novel.

I saw nothing wrong with those ambitions then.
This is nearly forty years later, and truth to tell, although my expectations are considerably diminished, I don't see anything wrong with them now!

THE RIGHT TO
ORGANIZE

WHILE A MAJOR portion of Dad's concern in 1934 was centered on his hopes for my year at Harvard, that same year began a new phase of his life in Dallas.

Starting in 1934, labor began sporadic efforts to organize Dallas. The Dallas open shop fought back with a will. Dallas had a booming nonunion garment industry which was a thorn in the side of the International Ladies Garment Workers Union. Leah Oleve, the first industrial union organizer to attempt to dent the Dallas open shop, was from the ILGWU. Dad was her first contact in Dallas, and for a time she used his office as her base.

The garment union's organizing drive had quick success among the young women who worked in the Dallas shops. The employers decided to resist any unionization. Collectively they refused all bargaining. Individual companies fired the most active of the union leaders in their shops. The ILGWU was faced with the choice of striking or leaving Dallas in abject defeat. It struck.

A substantial majority of the garment workers left their jobs, and the plants perforce closed down.

Soon, however, the employers began to resume operations and to hire new employees to take the places of those on strike. The question of loyalty to the company or loyalty to the union tore many families apart. The hatred between unionists and "scabs" engendered bitterness and violence on the picket line. Dad defended many of the picketers who were arrested, and on one day walked on a prohibited sidewalk himself and was arrested. He was never prosecuted. The prosecuting attorney explained his reluctance to press the charges not by relying on the First Amendment, but by saying, "I'm not going to let George Clifton Edwards make a monkey out of me."

The ILGWU effort in Dallas was a couple of years ahead of the great wave of industrial unionism, and it failed. The strike was broken and many of the most vigorous trade unionists were driven out of the Dallas garment industry.

Dad's persistence against odds and defeats was legendary. One story from this period may tell something of his stubbornness in dissent and his insistence on recording it.

One morning at breakfast he asked Nicky, who had just finished the *Dallas Morning News,* if she had seen his picture. Such an unlikely event pricked her interest, and she promptly did a careful scan of her paper. It was unsuccessful, and she reported that fact. Dad said, "Well, its there." Nicky went back to the search. This time page by page and with attention to the topics. On an inside page the

News had devoted a lot of space to a "citizen's in-
dignation" meeting against a labor-union organizing campaign. At some point the chairman had
called upon the protesters to express their resent-
ment against the invasion by "outside agitators" by
adopting a resolution by a rising vote. The picture
of the mass meeting, with the antilabor demon-
strators standing and cheering, was marred by a hat
on the crossed legs of just one firmly seated dis-
senter. The face was not visible, but a lot of people
in Dallas were able to identify the owner of the hat.

Starting in 1936 industrial unions under the
leadership of the Committee for Industrial Organization won some surprising victories—first in Akron
in the rubber industry, and then in the automobile
plants in Detroit.

I had gone to Detroit in 1936 to get a job in the
automobile industry and hopefully to write a novel
about it. I got the job all right, but I never wrote the
first line of the novel. I was caught up almost immediately in the astonishing revolution of the auto
workers against long hours, production-line speed,
and, above all, the callous use and discard of human
beings when they passed their physical peak. Auto
workers in '36 were frequently fired at forty-five
because they were too old for the job.

For three years I was an active part of the effort
of the United Automobile Workers to build a union
and shared in the rigors, the dangers, the exhilara-
tion—and the success. Dad lived my experiences
vicariously and saved every Detroit letter and

newspaper story for the entire period. But he was also personally involved in the repercussion of national UAW activities in the much more hostile atmosphere of Dallas.

After General Motors and Chrysler had signed collective-bargaining contracts with the UAW, the Ford Motor Company remained the major holdout in the automobile industry.

There was a Ford plant in Dallas. It was a final-assembly plant that produced Fords that were advertised as "Made in Texas by Texas Labor." No matter how remote it was from the center of the UAW-Ford conflict, the Dallas Ford plant produced some of the most unsavory pages of American labor history.

By 1937 Dad had moved his office from the North Texas Building to a second-story office over a store front on Commerce Street. His explanation to me was simple. For the same rent he got as much office space plus a meeting hall behind the office in case anyone might want to organize a meeting. In those early days itinerant unionists traveling through Dallas made a stop at Dad's office to brush up on the local scene and collect a free meal and, frequently, lodging for the night.

After the ILGWU experience in failing to breach the Dallas open-shop walls, no major industrial unions made any serious effort to organize a major industry in Dallas for some years. But the late thirties was a period when union organization was epidemic. In many instances it spread without plan.

Ford, under the domination of personnel director Harry Bennett, was taking no chances—in either Detroit or Dallas. In no place in the country was the Bennett system more clearly demonstrated (and ultimately more thoroughly exposed) than in Dallas.

In June, July, and August of 1937 a squad of Ford employees roamed Dallas looking and listening for evidence of organizational efforts or union sympathy. The slightest suspicion of either was sufficient to get the sympathizer a brutal beating. There were over fifty such assaults in the summer of 1937. Most of the victims had nothing at all to do with the UAW. One of these victims died within six months after the beating. On his deathbed he attributed his impending death to the Ford organized assault.

The violence started in June. Two men who were UAW members (one a local officer) at the Ford assembly plant in Kansas City stopped in Dallas on their vacations to see how Dallas Ford workers felt about unions. One of them, Baron DeLouis, was beaten up twice and driven out of Dallas. An attorney whom DeLouis had consulted, W. J. Houston, was attacked on Main Street in downtown Dallas by a gang of a dozen men, knocked to the ground, kicked repeatedly, and suffered three broken ribs.

The man who died was Archie B. Lewis. He was attacked by the Ford strong-arm squad at a wrestling match when he was mistaken for his twin brother, A. C. Lewis. Neither Lewis was any kin to John L. Lewis—indeed, neither had any union connection of any kind. A. C. Lewis, however, had committed the indiscretion of openly expressing a favorable view on unions.

At the very height of this terror I came home to Dallas for the briefest of vacations—three or four days, including my birthday on August 6, 1937. I also had instructions from the UAW, for which I then worked, to make a report on the prospects for organization of the Dallas Ford plant. In exchange I was to get my railroad coach fare paid. That year in Detroit had been so eventful and so full of tension that I greeted the chance to go to Dallas with enthusiasm. I knew of the trouble there, but since my work would hopefully be conducted quietly, I was not greatly concerned.

I took some precautions. Very few people in Detroit knew I was going, and in Dallas only Dad knew that I was coming home. We arranged for him to meet me at the last railroad station before the train arrived in Dallas. I must say that I looked up and down the Highland Park station platform with some concern before deciding that it was empty— aside from Dad.

When we got into the car, Dad expressed his fears for me and I for him. He then asked me if I wanted a pistol while I was in Dallas. I assured him that that was the last thing I wanted around. He seemed relieved.

The several days I spent there passed quickly and uneventfully. I saw a good many people— carefully avoiding any previously arranged appointments—and I got a thorough grounding in how the Dallas Ford plant was going about forestalling labor-union organization. More important from the point of view of my report, I also confirmed what I had previously been told—that the Dallas plant was exclusively final assembly. This meant, of course, that if Dallas were organized ahead of the Rouge complex and other Ford assembly plants, the union would be dangerously vulnerable. A shutdown by strike or lockout in Dallas would mean only minimal economic pressure on the company, but would mean nothing short of disaster to the employees and their union. It would be hard to argue for diverting manpower or money from the main effort to organize the important Ford plants in Michigan to deal with the Ford Dallas terror. It wasn't a pleasant conclusion, in view of the engagement of my family and friends in Dallas.

I left Dallas the night of August 6 after a pleasant visit and without having heard a hostile word or seen a hostile gesture. I never knew until I started to write this book that the brutal beating of Archie B. Lewis, which apparently led to his death, occurred on August 4, 1937, the second night of my brief visit. Strangely, I felt that I was leaving a peaceful haven and was heading back to the maelstrom that was Detroit of 1937. Obviously, this was not entirely the case.

Actually, the Ford terror reached its peak in Dallas that week end. The Dallas police had done little or nothing to prevent the preceding assaults or to prosecute the perpetrators. Indeed, there was evidence they sanctioned some of them. But there were efforts to resist and to counter the violence.

One of these was a meeting on Saturday afternoon, August 8, at the Dallas city hall. Dad helped to organize it, and he was chairman of the meeting. The campaign of terror just referred to was described and denounced. A labor film, *Millions of Us,* published by the Textile Workers Organizing Committee, was shown. At the meeting, which apparently was attended by Ford agents, plans were announced for a meeting in Fretz Park the following evening.

What happened beforehand at that Monday night meeting in the park is told most authoritatively in the words of the official decision of the National Labor Relations Board, entered August 8, 1940. As to this decision the United States Court of Appeals for the Fifth Circuit was later to comment: "The findings of the Board were not only supported by substantial evidence, they were compelled by it."

In few labor cases was the evidence ever so clear. Most of the witnesses (such as "Fats" Perry, Worley, Dill, Hill, and Bevill) were the former Ford strong-arm men (by then discharged by Ford) who had themselves perpetrated the assaults. They testified with utmost frankness about what they had done and who (like Ford plant supervisor Rutland in the following quote) had ordered them to do it.

The decision describes that Monday in the park as follows:

A second showing [of the film *Millions of Us*] at an open meeting at a public park was advertised for the following evening. During the morning of August 9 Perry discussed the proposed showing at the park with Rutland who instructed him to demolish the film while it was being shown if it was a C.I.O. picture or portrayed a union organizer. Perry thereafter made arrangements with the park policeman for the disruption of the meeting and the destruction of the film. At the close of work that afternoon Claud Dill called a meeting of several hundred employees and members of inside squads for the purpose of coordinating their functions with those of the outside squad. Dill and Worley addressed the gathering, Dill instructing them to go to the park and to start breaking up the meeting when he gave the word. The group captains received more specific directions, and Beck's role was to stand beside Dill and heckle the speaker until the general signal to advance was indicated. That afternoon while he was at work on the assembly line at the plant, Longley was instructed by Hill, a member of the outside squad and in charge of some of the inside squads, to notify all members of the inside group of which he was captain to attend a meeting at Hill's home at a designated hour in the early evening. When the group assembled at his house, Hill opened the meeting with the statement that there was to be a showing that night of a moving picture on union activity at one of the city parks, to be followed immediately by an address. He then informed the meeting that all the groups would be present at the park; that one group had been specially assigned to breaking up the meeting and to protecting the women and children; and that the members of this particular group had also been selected to go down there on special assignment. Longley was to get the sound records and one or

two others were to see that he was not molested in the
performance of this task. The question of wrecking the
projection machine was also discussed. Hill himself was
to tar and feather the speaker.

All groups proceeded to the park for the showing and
remained silently at their posts until it was over. When a
speaker began to address the crowd, he was heckled by
those who had been planted in the audience for that purpose, one of the questions asked of him being whether
the film could be rented by the C.I.O. His affirmative
reply brought the order "Tear it up, boys!" from Dill and
the planned disruption of the meeting and demolition of
the film and other equipment ensued. In accordance
with prior arrangements, Longley seized the sound
records and took them to Rutland's home, after visiting
the plant and finding that Rutland was not there. Rutland
directed Longley to remove the records from his home
and to destroy them, as he was afraid that they might
otherwise be discovered in Rutland's possession. Longley followed Rutland's instructions. Hill executed his assignment that evening by seizing, instead of the speaker
whom he considered too old, Herbert Harris, the projec-
tionist, whom he transported under a blindfold to one of
the usual whipping places, after beating him into insen-
sibility. Perry and other members of his squad, who were
present at the whipping place after Hill and Harris arrived, ordered Harris to remove most of his clothing and
applied to his body two coats of a tar-like substance
which they had acquired at the plant. They then covered
with feathers the coating he had received, put him back
in the automobile in which Hill had transported him, and
took him into town, leaving him behind the Dallas News
building. The usual procedure of directing their victims
to leave town immediately was not followed in this instance, as Fleet Hall and Ray Martin had made arrangements in advance of the tarring and feathering with a
photographer for the Dallas News, a daily newspaper, for

the photographing of Harris in his coat of tar and feathers. When the automobile drove away from the spot at which he had been left behind the Dallas News building, Harris jerked off the blindfold and called for help. A crowd gathered, the police arrived, and photographs were taken of Harris, whom one of Perry's men described as a "bird" after he had been tarred and feathered. Worley and another member of the outside squad returned to the plant and talked with Rutland who had returned there from his home. An employee on duty at the time as relief watchman in the employment office heard Rutland say to them laughingly, "Well, you boys did a damn good job of it." Early the following morning Dill handed one of the watchmen at the plant, who testified without contradiction and credibly, a folded paper, instructing him to give it to Abbott and explaining to the watchman that it contained a specimen of the tar and feathers used the previous evening. The watchman turned it over to Abbott. Perry, Longley, Beck, Bevill, and others whose testimony we believe testified without contradiction as to the various aspects of the activities of the inside and outside squads in connection with this public meeting and as to the role played by Rutland.

That same day Ford agents kidnaped and beat nearly to death still another man who had no connection with the UAW, the CIO, or the Ford plant. This one was a unionist named George Baer. He was an organizer for the Hat, Cap and Millinery Workers of the American Federation of Labor (then sharply divided from the CIO) and had been in Dallas as a representative of that union since April, 1936. On August 6, 1937, he made an appointment to talk about collective bargaining with Mike Bierner, owner of a millinery shop. Rudolph Rutland, the Ford plant supervisor who had active charge of the antiunion violence, received a call about the Baer appointment. He sent two of his strong-arm crew to talk to Dallas police officials about Baer. The same two men then arranged for and participated in trapping Baer at an appointment with Bierner on Sunday, August 9, 1937. They kidnaped him at gunpoint, blackjacked him mercilessly, and ultimately left him, near death, unconscious in an open field. Taken to a hospital, Baer recovered very slowly from his wounds. One eye had been put out. The beating and the loss of the eye had made an old man out of a vigorous young man.

One of the Ford agents who participated in this attack gave this revealing testimony:

Q. After you saw Mr. Baer there pretty badly beaten up with Mr. Johnson in the car with him, what happened?
A. I walked over to the car and opened the door, Mr. Johnson got out and I reached in and got Mr. Baer and pulled him out; pulled him out on the ground. I asked him, I said, "Do you know who you are?" He said, "Oh, you got the wrong man. You have got the wrong man. You got the wrong man." I said, "No, we haven't got the wrong man. We got the right duck." I says, "Who sent you to this town?" He repeated himself, "You got the wrong man. You got the wrong man. You got the wrong man." I said, "Well, the man isn't going to talk. Take him down there and dump him in the river and you can talk to him." I said, "Do you understand what I am talking about." He said, "Yes, I understand what you are talking about." I said, "What is your name?" He said, "My name is Mr. Baer." I said, "Who sent you to this town?" He

said, "I came from Boston, Massachusetts," or some place in the East, I am not positive. I said, "You are hurt pretty bad, aren't you?" He said, "Yes, I am hurt pretty bad." I said, "You are not hurt so bad you don't know what you are talking about." He said, "No, sir, I am not hurt so bad I don't know what I am talking about." I said, "Who sent you here?" He said, "I don't know, men. I am beat up pretty bad. I don't know just exactly what I am saying, but I would like for you men to leave me alone." I said, "We are going to leave you alone, and you are not going to be hurt no more if you get out of this town." He said, "Well, I will go. I will leave."

Of the Ford strong-arm crew who disrupted the park meeting and beat up and tarred and feathered Herbert Harris and beat George Baer nearly to death, none was arrested. But one of the victims of the assaults in the park was. George Lambert, a Dallas man and labor unionist, tried to stop the destruction of the movie projector and was repeatedly struck on the face and head. The park police arrested him, and Dad had to go to the city jail to secure his release on bail. Dad and Carl Brannin also took charge of Herbert Harris and kept him in hiding in their homes during this period. As the Ford agents had obviously planned, the next day's *Dallas News* printed the picture of Herbert Harris tarred and feathered. There was also a picture of Baer in a hospital bed showing the effects of the beating he had received. The terror (and the advertising of it) were designed, of course, to scare people away from joining or supporting unions. But in this instance it had a somewhat opposite effect. Whether as a result of such visible evidence of lawlessness or of the efforts of Dad and others to secure help, Governor Allred intervened by sending a detachment of Texas rangers to Dallas. In spite of protests of the mayor, the police chief, and the Ford officials, the rangers remained in Dallas and were frequently thereafter on hand to forestall further attacks.

Dad's diary for late August records a visit—unproductive—to the Dallas county grand jury with Herbert Harris, George Lambert, and Carl Brannin; a conference with L. N. D. Wells, Jr., counsel for the National Labor Relations Board; a "very good meeting at City Park," where Carl Brannin, Herbert Harris, and George Lambert "spoke well"; a letter to the *Dallas News* on the Ford terror and public authority's failure to stop it or prosecute the perpetrators.

In early September Dad was busy organizing a meeting, under the auspices of the Texas Workers Defense League, at which Norman Thomas was to speak about the breakdown of law and order. At the meeting Dad introduced Thomas, making reference to Thomas's courage in his then recent successful efforts to restore freedom of speech in Boss Hague's bastion of Jersey City. Thomas responded by pointing out that usually his contribution was a one-night stand where the most he could do was to state a position. "The real heroes," he said, "are those like George Clifton Edwards who live in the midst of the terror and continue to resist oppression."

Dad's diary for early September, 1937, contains these entries:

Sept. 9   Spoke at Thomas meeting. Hardly slept!

Sept. 10   Arranged for Herbert Harris to get out of town.

Sept. 15   Ford gangsters lay in wait to attack someone at our meeting, but left when we called the Rangers—who followed Brannin and me home.

Sept. 19   Spoke at meeting on "The Constitution—Bulwark to Liberty." Rangers and police on guard.

Sept. 21   Phone call from abusive and threatening thug who "is going to stomp my brains out" if I or Lambert or Brannin print anything more.

The last comment had been provoked by one of Dad's not infrequent letters to the *Dallas Morning News:*

> The lawyers and the Bar Association of Dallas are strangely silent just now at a time when it would seem that courage, conscience, and principle ought to make them speak vigorously. It is no exaggeration to state that in Dallas mob disregard for law and mob destruction of men's constitutional rights have made Dallas a byword and a scoffing with those who seriously care for justice, peace and order. Man after man, violating no law, attending to his own affairs peaceably, has been attacked and beaten by mobs. The police make no arrests, and the prosecutors sit at ease in their well-paid offices, undisturbed. Twice in the heart of the city, in open daylight, during business hours when the streets were thronged, citizens have been beset with mobs and kidnapers, and the police are everywhere, it seems, but near those crowded districts. A public meeting, violating no law, is ganged by organized thugs, property is destroyed worth hundreds of dollars, one man is slugged and

left for dead, another kidnaped, tarred and
feathered. Not one of these victims was doing
anything illegal. All were acting within their
specific legal rights. Yet our huge, expensive,
heavily armed police department, with scores
of detectives, professes to be at its wits' end.

The lawyers of Dallas who are experienced
and sophisticated enough to appreciate the
farce the law enforcing (God save the mark)
officers are playing, are strangely silent.

If Dallas lawyers revere the Constitution,
they ought most especially to revere the bill of
rights, and the first article thereof. For it is
simply a historical fact that without the bill of
rights the Federal Constitution would not
have been adopted. Without the definite
pledge for the bill of rights, in due time made
good, we would not have the Constitution.
The critical and all-important first article guar-
antees freedom of speech and freedom of assembly. The Texas bill of rights is even more
definite and detailed.

It seems to me that now, if ever, there is
need for a resounding protest by all lawyers
who are sincere in their concern over the Constitution and its basis, the bill of rights. Dallas
lawyers ought to speak out and to rouse the
public to the dangers threatening our constitutional rights. They ought to help stir the police
department and the prosecuting authorities
into doing something beyond talking and stall-
ing, as they are doing during this mob violence
in Dallas.

The Ford terror ceased toward the end of 1937.
Just why is a matter of speculation, since the Bennett regime was still very much in charge of Ford
policy. The rangers' presence certainly was a factor

and evoked some bitter attacks on Governor Allred. The *Dallas News* finally editorialized against mob violence, which damaged the "good name" of Dallas. Perhaps, finally, the Dallas Ford management came to realize that in fact there was not (and never had been) any serious effort being made to organize the Dallas plant. Perhaps someplace in the background was some awareness of the National Labor Relations Board.

The National Labor Relations Act became effective in July, 1935. The board moved slowly in choosing staff and beginning its work of policing the newly created statutory right for working men to organize and bargain through unions of their own choosing. In Texas a distinguished university professor from Texas Christian University, Dr. Edwin Elliott, was chosen as regional director. An articulate young lawyer, L. N. D. Wells, Jr., was chosen as counsel for the board. He was one of many Dallasites of a younger generation who attributed much of the inspiration of their work to my father. The Ford terror laid down the most direct sort of challenge to Elliott and Wells, and they met it.

Wells had had easy access, of course, to the victims of the terror. But few of them could do much toward identifying their assailants, let alone tying them by direct evidence to the Ford Motor Company. In 1939, however, the Dallas Ford plant saw fit to fire a number of the leaders of the 1937 mob violence. These men, who had themselves perpetrated the attacks, were called to the witness stand

and under oath described the beatings they had
planned and administered and testified, in addition,
as to which of the Dallas Ford supervisory force had
directed them to do so.

Baron DeLouis, the twice-badly-beaten officer
of the Kansas City UAW local, had the satisfaction of
representing the United Automobile Workers at the
lengthy hearings in Dallas in 1940.

Few records of company-organized antiunion violence are as complete or as dramatic or resulted in
as sweeping an order to cease and desist as In the
Matter of Ford Motor Co., 26 N.L.R.B. 34 (1940).

The decision of the board was released August
8, 1940. It doubtless helped make the organization
of the Dallas Ford plant possible. But the organization of the Rouge complex in Detroit and the signing of a national agreement between Ford and the
UAW one year later probably had even more to do
with the fact that the Dallas Ford workers finally got
to belong to a union.

FAMILY VISITS –
PRE-WORLD WAR II

LIKE MOST FAMILIES that are separated by geography, ours made much of the opportunities we got for family visits. There was much history of living in two different cities to catch up on. Again, however, there were differences. Our visiting tended to center around events or occasions and not just around holidays. The difference is easy to illustrate.

Dad's first visit to Detroit was in the spring of 1938. We met briefly three times in the Wayne County jail, where I was serving a thirty-day sentence for violation of an injunction. This episode requires reference to some history. Until the 1940s (and sometimes after) the American labor movement's attempts to organize frequently had been met by illegal, although often officially sanctioned, violence. The Ford Dallas plant violence was only an example of a quite general practice, which included the shooting of strikers on the fields outside the Republic Steel plant at South Chicago in 1937, and still earlier company-inspired violence in the Ludlow massacre of 1914 in the Colorado Fuel and

Iron Company strike and in the strike at the Homestead Works of Carnegie Steel in 1892.

When Congress adopted the National Labor Relations Act, it formally declared the right to organize and required employers to bargain with unions chosen by their employees. Promptly American industry, through the Liberty League, answered that it considered the NLRA unconstitutional and that industry would not obey it. The answer to the Liberty League that the Committee for Industrial Organization (CIO) adopted was the sit-down strike, a tactic widely used for several years.

Sit-down strikes were bitterly condemned by industry as illegal seizures of private property. Labor spokesmen and their lawyers, however, argued that where the company concerned had previously defied the law of the land, the sit-down strike was a legally permissible remedy. In any event, their argument continued, a company that refused collective bargaining came into court with unclean hands and should not be entitled to injunctive relief. We now know, of course, that these arguments were rejected by the United States Supreme Court's decision in the *Fansteel* case. But that decision did not come until some years later, in 1939.

In Michigan the first major strikes in the thirties at General Motors and Chrysler brought no court test of these disputed theories. Gov. Frank Murphy talked the strikers into leaving the plants by securing a commitment from the companies that they would negotiate and would not try to operate.

During the massive Chrysler sit-down strike in the early part of 1937 there was another strike so insignificant that few people knew it was happening. It was at a plant of a Chrysler supplier, the Yale & Towne Lock Company, on the northwest side of Detroit. No one had tried to organize Yale & Towne. The largely young female employee group had organized itself and then called the union for help. The call went to the West Side Local of the UAW, of which Walter Reuther was then the president. I was the union representative who got the call.

The Yale & Towne girls assembled locks for Chrysler. They had all the grievances the male employees had, and quite a few that applied only to them. The former included complaints about low wages, no seniority, and speed-up. The latter included repeated and heated complaints about being forced to go out with and submit to the attentions of the male foremen. As the Chrysler strike curtailed Yale & Towne operations, the company began to lay off first (and without regard to seniority) the girls who had been the leaders of the organization of the plant. Absent negotiations, a strike was inevitable. The company refused, point-blank, to set up any meeting with the union committee. A sit-down strike began.

With 100,000 workers on strike at the Chrysler plants, the state and national stake in a peaceful settlement of that strike was very great. Finally, as indicated above, the Chrysler strike was settled. But

the Yale & Towne strike went on. The local management told us that they wanted to negotiate—but
nationally Yale & Towne had an adamant antiunion policy. The parent corporation, based at
Stamford, Connecticut, had successfully resisted
labor organization in its plants and flatly withstood
all efforts to get it to the bargaining table—law or no
law.

Suddenly, and without notice, the company
went to Judge Arthur Webster, an able, very conservative Wayne County circuit judge, and procured a
restraining order requiring the strikers to leave the
Yale & Towne plant.

Redoubled efforts to secure the sort of truce that
had resulted in termination of the General Motors
and Chrysler strikes were still going on when one
afternoon four hundred policemen and sheriff's
deputies arrived at the plant, fired dozens of rounds
of tear-gas shells into it, and arrested all the people
who were there, including me. A number of us were
charged, tried, and found guilty of contempt of
court. I received the longest sentence—thirty days.

There was no doubt that the restraining order
had not been obeyed, and doubtless once it had
been issued the judge had a duty to enforce it. At
the Senate hearing on my confirmation Senator
Dirksen read a paragraph from Judge Webster's
statement at the contempt hearing, describing the
judge's duty to enforce his order. Dirksen asked me
what I thought about it and seemed surprised when
I answered that leaving Judge Webster's adjectives

aside I thought he was right. Of course, whether he should have issued it without trying to settle the dispute is another matter. These thoughts are, however, the long, subsequent thoughts of a lawyer and a judge. But even at twenty-two, when I was neither lawyer nor judge, the legal arguments in court at the contempt hearing gave me no optimism about appealing the sentences. My reaction, and that of the other strike leaders who were similarly sentenced, was simply to serve them.

Dad had had no part in any of this except to send a telegram the night we were arrested. It read, "Take a bath, get a night's sleep and clean shirt, and go back to work, toujours l'audace." But a few days after I had started to serve the sentence, Frank Winn, with whom I then shared a couple of rooms [in downtown Detroit] came by the jail to tell me that Dad was coming to Detroit. Frank's recollections of that event tell something of Dad's persistence and of his ability to survive under adversity:

When your father came to Detroit after you had been sentenced to jail by Judge Webster, I went to meet him at the train, which arrived at about ten at night. Before I went to the Michigan Central station, I went by the jail and talked to a deputy about Mr. Edwards's seeing you as soon as we could get to the jail after he arrived. "No chance," he said. "Far too late." I explained that Mr. Edwards was an attorney, but he was adamant. Your father would have to wait until the next day.

The train came in on time. He had come by day coach and, as I remember, the trip was two days and a night. He said he would like a bite to eat at the lunch counter—a piece of pie and a glass of milk. While he ate I told him of my fruitless efforts to arrange for him to see you that night. I said I knew he was tired and proposed that I take him directly to the apartment—Alfred Street, God save the mark!—and I would take him to the jail first thing in the morning.

He listened in silence while he ate his pie and made no comment at all of assent or dissent until we got up from the counter and started out of the station. Then he said: "Frank, if you'll show me where to catch the right streetcar, I'll go on down to the jail. I want to go there to-night."

I said of course if he wanted to go I would take him there, but I didn't think it would do any good.

When we went into the jail building the same deputy was at the counter.

"This is Mr. Edwards," I said. "He wants to see George tonight."

"Absolutely impossible. It's way past visiting hours. Nobody can see prisoners at this time of night."

Then your father said quite calmly but firmly: "I am not only George's father; I'm his attorney. I want to see my client."

The deputy looked at me in exasperation, but shrugged his shoulders and shook his head in a helpless "what can you do?" attitude, came around the corner from behind the counter, let your father in that visiting room, and went to get you. Once your father spoke, there was no further argument. I am sure he was within his rights and the deputy knew it, but I don't think any other attorney could have seen his client under those circumstances without using a lot more words and a much louder voice.

Actually I remember little about that visit except that it happened and that Dad was bound to see Judge Webster and Governor Murphy. I saw little prospect in either mission.

The next afternoon Dad was back at the jail. He

had seen Judge Webster, and the judge was willing
to release me if I would ask for the release and
tender a public apology. I felt that the Yale & Town
strikers had been much more sinned against than
sinning and that my apology would be understood
as reflecting on them and their cause. I declined.

Dad didn't argue. He simply said that he would
tell Judge Webster my decision and that he would
be going to Lansing the next morning to see Governor Murphy.

He was back the following evening to report failure. He had seen the governor and his legal adviser
for an hour. It was, I gathered, a friendly interview,
but both the legal adviser and the governor took the
position that the contempt sentence I was serving
was a civil rather than a criminal commitment and
not subject to gubernatorial pardoning power. Dad
took a night train to Dallas. He had been in Detroit
less than forty-eight hours.

I caught up on a good deal of reading and a good
deal of sleeping in the Wayne County jail.

Seventeen years later, in 1954, I was sworn in as
a judge in the Wayne County Circuit Court. Judge
Webster was still on that bench. Much water had
flowed under many bridges by then. By mutual
agreement he held my robe when I took the bench.

One episode during Dad's visit has stuck in my
mind vividly ever since. The sheriff of Wayne
County at the time was Tom Wilcox. He was a Dem-
ocrat and I suspect most unhappy about the role that
he had to play at Yale & Towne. The sheriff also ran

the jail and Wilcox lived in an apartment in the jail. He was probably not very happy about being my jailer either.

In any event, the day Dad went to see Judge Webster, the sheriff came around to see me. He talked about Dad's visit and his coming all the way from Texas and said that it would be too bad if Dad and I could only see each other in the jail. He ended up telling me that he would have a deputy take me out under guard and meet Dad at a restaurant for dinner. I expressed some doubts about the idea, but he assured me it was perfectly legal since I would be in his custody all the while and would be back in the jail within a couple of hours. He had picked a deputy with whom I had struck up a friendship and had already gotten his agreement. The notion of relief from jail food even for one meal was certainly tempting. I agreed.

At the appointed hour my deputy friend showed up, unlocked the door, and led me out through basement corridors and a back door to the jail building that I had never seen before. He had a car nearby, and we got to the restaurant where Dad was to be without any incident.

At the door to the restaurant the deputy, to my consternation, told me he had some things he wanted to do, that I could have dinner with Dad alone and come back to the jail by myself to the same door by which we had left. I should ring the bell right at ten o'clock and he would be there to let me in. If I was doubtful about the sheriff's proposal

I was ten times more worried about this. I protested vehemently but without making any impression. I gathered that the deputy had a date and was already late for it. He drove off laughing.

I didn't find Dad in a mood for laughter when I joined him in the restaurant. He was as concerned as I, or more so. He had known nothing of the dinner scheme until he returned from Lansing and Frank Winn told him—too late to register any opinion on the matter. We shared an uneasy couple of hours together during which he told me of his visit with the governor. Then he left to catch his train back to Dallas and I to return to the jail.

I walked back to the jail through the downtown area feeling like one of the FBI's ten most wanted men. No one paid me the slightest attention. I reached Gratiot at a point behind the Wayne County jail well before 10:00 P.M. There was the door, across a well-lighted, vacant field that looked to me as big as a football field. Finally, feeling more conspicuous than ever in my life, I made myself walk directly across the open area to the back door and ring the bell. It was a couple of minutes before ten. Nothing happened. I waited and rang again. Nothing happened. The minutes of waiting were agony. Finally, at several minutes after ten, I left, resuming an aimless wandering around nearby blocks. I thought of every possible alternative, all to no good purpose. Many people must have spent time trying to figure out how to break out of that jail. I spent some trying to figure how to get into

it. I could of course go back in the main entrance to
the jail but I felt that doing that was sure to get my
deputy friend into all sorts of trouble. At 10:15 I
was back at the door, ringing the bell again. The
experience was just as agonizing as before and just
as fruitless. Again, the aimless wandering and worrying, and at 10:30 I was back at the door. I rang,
the door opened, there was the deputy. I doubt that
many men have ever been as thankful to find themselves in a jail bunk as I was that night.

The sheriff may not have known that I was ever
out of technical custody, but his unsolicited leave of
absence was not rewarded by much gratitude. My
memory of the episode was much too full of anxiety.
And the memory was still vivid a few years later
when Wilcox was convicted of betraying his public
trust by taking money from racketeers.

The next visit to Detroit from a member of my
family came in April, 1939. My sister, Nicky, came
to see Peg and me married. Mother and Dad
couldn't—or didn't come. In various ways they sent
their blessings and their good wishes; and if doubts
or fears helped keep them away, they did not mention them. As it was, we were surrounded by
enough of such.

My memory of the beauty of spring in Texas was
partly responsible for the April date for the wedding. In Detroit that year on April 10 it rained,
snowed, and sleeted. The weather outside was a
good backdrop for the mood of most who gathered
at the McConnell home for the wedding. In Peg

McConnell's world her marriage to me was seen not
merely as a social disaster. In the midst of the labor-
management conflict that had torn Michigan apart,
it was received as something akin to treason.

Peg's father, Rollin McConnell, was a prominent
stockbroker in Detroit, numbering many of the
leaders of the automobile industry among his
clients. The two daughters of the family grew up in
the social activity of the Detroit Golf Club and the
Detroit Athletic Club. The year before our marriage
Peg's younger sister Flo had married Semon Knudsen, the only son of William S. Knudsen, president
of the General Motors Corporation. Their wedding
had been the social event of the year.

There were only two people in the world who
had known both Peg and me. Both had met Peg
when she was at Connecticut College at New London. Both knew me through the LID. Both tried to
introduce us, and one succeeded. His description of
Peg McConnell had left me anything but enthusiastic about spending a summer Sunday afternoon
meeting her. "Big wheel on the campus," he said.
"President of student government—dean's list—
government major—a real liberal—led the Connecticut College students on the Electric Boat Company picket line two years ago."

I envisioned an intense young woman, with
horn-rimmed glasses, weighing, say, 150 pounds.
What I saw was a lovely girl curled up in a big arm
chair in her family's living room. When she stood up
to greet us, she was a little over 5 feet tall and

weighed 100 pounds. The brightly striped house-
coat she was wearing set off a figure that made me
catch my breath. She had laughing eyes that looked
directly at you. She spoke easily and frankly. She
was interested and she listened. She was the easiest
person to like whom I had ever met. By the time I
left the house, I had asked her for a date. I had also
decided that this might be the girl I wanted to
marry—if she would have me.

Our six-month courtship isn't part of this story,
but the reconciliation of our families to the marriage
is. Our abrupt announcement to Peg's father that we
were going to get married must have been the shock
of his life. He hardly knew me, and Peg, at that
time, was thought likely to marry a young man with
whom she had been going for several years. Before
a year passed, Mac's great affection for his indepen-
dent-minded daughter had encompassed me. Since
we were both in downtown Detroit, we saw a good
deal of each other. In my city-government days (and
later) Mac was a strong supporter—in spite of
locker-room arguments with his DAC and golf club
friends. He and Peg's sister, Florence, through
warmth and love (and some diplomacy), bridged the
family gap of differing convictions.

My family, of course, did not know Peg, and I
fear my descriptions were most inadequate. They
did, of course, know that Peg's family had objected
to our marriage. In the summer of 1939 Peg and I
went to Dallas, and she met Dad and Mother for the
first time. She had already won their hearts by her

letters—far more frequent and newsy than mine had ever been. In person she won them as quickly and completely as she had me. Octavia Crump gave Peg the final family accolade. The first day she met Peg, Octavia took me aside and said, "George, I sure do like your Peggy. Why, she's just as plain as plain can be."

Dad's second visit to Detroit involved somewhat less drama than the first. He came in midwinter without Mother to see me sworn in as a newly elected member of the Detroit city council. Afterward, by letter from Dallas, he indulged in the longest bit of paternal advice I ever received:

Dear Son:

For all the fact that we have always been devoted to each other, I find it hard to talk to you about serious and intimate matters across the years, and in cold type. But I will try, and you will know that anything that I may say that is inept comes out of some other defect of mine than a lack of love and devotion to you and your family and your future.

(There follows a paragraph that can only be excused by paternal affection and is excluded here on the grounds that it would be self-serving testimony from a highly prejudiced witness.) Dad continued:

But your great chance has also great danger. I mention it and look to your good judgment to save you from it. It is the danger of either being forced into a permanent minority of one, where you can do nothing for the people and your ideals except make a protest; or of being led into a sinking of the workers' interests into a compliance with the majority so that your real purposes cannot be realized. That 8–1 vote on the pay raise is an illustration

of the way things work. You have got so to conduct your
affairs that they cannot brand you as a "mere" labor man,
whom they can and will invariably vote down when any
important matter is at stake; and yet you have likewise so
to conduct yourself that the council will know uncon-
sciously, and instinctively, that there is one man on it
who is devoted to the interests of the workers and of the
people and not to mere politics or personal advantage.
You have got to find some way to get along with the
members so that they will not hesitate to vote with you,
and vote with you even when they know that you are
leading. You have an unusual ability to make friends and
to avoid useless antagonism. I hope you can find the best
side and the best characteristics of every one of the council and make them realize that you are co-operating with
them in the very acts and motions and votes when you
are looking after the interests of the workers, who are the
great mass, whom we want to help and to serve. In other
words I want you to win friends and supporters in the
council so that you will not be "horned off" and made
ineffective as I have been in Dallas. . . . If you can win
friends and supporters in the council—and you certainly
have a fine start in the friendship of Jeffries and Lodge
[respectively the mayor and council president of De-
troit], and to my observation you have no one who does
not wish you well and at the same time hold to your
ideals and purposes in the labor movement, the future
looks good to me; and I am not prone to look too much on
the bright side.

Another thing. I am very anxious, directly in line with
the above remarks, for you to finish your law school work.
NOW is the time. And it all depends on whether you and
Peg have and can practice enough self-restraint and de-
termination to prevent all and sundry from using up all
your time, i.e. if you and Peg can *budget your time*. *NOW*
is your chance. For two years you are fairly secure of a
good living and of time to earn your pay AND ALSO to
do your reading. Do not gamble on the distant future.

NOW is the time to get that job of reading done. And it is a most important job for a man planning a career as a politician in the high and good sense. As a lawyer you will have an advantage that will help you greatly.

Still another thing. I hope you will proceed, with Peg to budget your expenses. Save some money. Not just to be saving some money. Save some money because if you have some money saved up you will have an independence that you cannot have any other way. The man who is in debt and worried by creditors, or even by debts that the creditors merely hold and never speak of, has a burden that will prevent him from the free exercise of his voice and vote and power in an incalculable way. I do not desire for you that you should "make money," but I do desire for you that you should be your own man, be independent of persons who can bring pressure to bear on you. . . .

And as I come near the end of this perhaps too solemn letter, I want to assure you that I have not forgotten the word we so often have used between us. *I do want* you to cultivate friendship and support in the council, cultivate EVERY ONE OF THEM, even the baseball player and the professional Mason. *I do want* you to study so that you will become the best informed man on the council both in theory and in practice. This will be quite possible. Most politicians do not study as the early Al Smith did. *I do want* you to be careful of your standard of expenditures and of your money so that the Philistines may not get a hold on you. *But I do want also* for you to remember that what has carried you through many hard situations and brought you to the place you are, with its glorious opportunities, is "l'audace, toujours l'audace."

Give my love to Peg, whom I highly approve of and appreciate, and to the little boy, who seems to me inexpressibly charming. YDF, G.C.E.

WORLD WAR II

IN SEPTEMBER, 1939, Hitler invaded Poland, and England and France declared war. As World War II exploded, Peg and I were in Dallas on her first visit to meet my family. Since 1933 the evidence that war was coming had been piling up. Dad's antiwar convictions of a lifetime were not easy to change, but Adolf Hitler overcame them.

From the days of the Munich beer hall *Putsch* Hitler had been anathema at the family dinner table. His rekindling of German militarism, his persecution of the Jews, his destruction of Germany's social democracy made his name synonymous in our household with human evil in its worst form. In addition, Dad took Hitler's burning of books as something akin to a personal affront. Still, as of 1934, the possibility of Hitler as a leader of world conquest had never crossed my mind, nor I think had it crossed Dad's. Germany was too weak. France and England were too strong. Hitler was too crazy. The American peace movement still made sense.

Successively, however, those of us who were ardent adherents of peace were compelled to watch while the Nazi planes and tanks and guns snuffed out liberty and democracy in Spain, in Austria, and in Czechoslovakia. This was naked force prevailing over reason, intelligence, and good will. I found myself utterly committed to the support of the brave men who fought against Hitler and for freedom in each of these lost causes. Soon I had to face the fact that my hopes for American noninvolvement rested entirely on the strength of arms of those nations in Europe that were still allied against Hitler. This was an increasingly tenuous hope, and I wanted America to bolster it.

At Munich I thought Chamberlain's strategy made no sense. Increasingly I had to recognize that the pacifist neutrality position made no sense either. There was no peaceful means to cope with Hitler.

Prior to Peggy's and my visit to Dallas in 1939, I had no certainty as to what had happened to Dad's thinking. To my considerable surprise that September I found him an interventionist, ready to send material aid to France and England—and weapons, too, if need be. Whatever the price was for the break with his beloved Socialist party, he was willing to pay it in order to live realistically in the world in which he found himself.

Once started, he went all the way. A year or so later, after Dunkirk, when I asked him how he felt about the lend-lease of American destroyers to hard-pressed England, Dad replied "We ought to send the American fleet to the British Channel."

All his life Dad abhorred violence as a solution to any human problem. Hitler did create a mon-

strous exception to this rule. There may have been
another, albeit of much smaller dimension.

One Sunday during the war Mother and Dad
had gone downtown to a meeting. Dad had stopped
by the office to pick up a large electric table fan.
They planned to take the Fairmount streetcar back
home. Their streetcar arrived, came to a stop, and
they started from the curb to board it. Dad had
Mother on his left arm and he held the electric fan
by its guard in the other hand. They had the right of
way legally and in practice in Dallas, but an approaching cab elected to disregard both. Dad saw
the cab coming. He pulled Mother, who was in the
path of the cab, back toward the curb. In the process
he turned and the base of the fan swung out and
shattered the cab's right headlight. The cab driver
jammed on his brakes, jumped from the cab, and
began profuse apologies. Dad received the apologies with dignity, assuring him (to his great relief)
that neither he nor Mother were injured. As they
boarded the car, the motorman said to Dad, "That
cabbie sure got what was coming to him." Dad
smiled but didn't answer. When they reached their
seats, Mother turned to him and said, "Georgie, you
did that on purpose." Dad never replied to that either.

The years of World War II following Pearl Harbor found Dad and Mother, like most Americans,
doing what they could for the war effort. By then
they had moved to a big, old frame house on University Boulevard, close to SMU. All during the war

its upstairs rooms were occupied by visiting soldiers—either friends of ours from Michigan or some soldiers (out of the thousands of recruits being trained in Texas army camps) sent to the family by the USO for lodging and a couple of home-cooked meals.

The tragedy of the war came home vividly and personally when Walter and Harry Crump were lost. And when I went into the army, Mother and Dad both took on responsibilities for mail call at my barracks and at our home in Detroit where Peggy was maintaining the home front with our two little boys.

With all of this, the concerns of other days were still present. There was a sort of unwritten truce during World War II between management and labor. The Texas legislature, however, was not a party to it and in 1943 it adopted a statute that the labor movement looked on as another sort of declaration of war.

The act purported generally to regulate labor unions, but specifically it required any labor organizer to apply to the secretary of state for an organizer's card and to carry it at all times when soliciting members for a union, on penalty of a $500 fine and sixty days in jail. With the Ford Dallas terror fresh in the minds of Texas unionists, advance registration and formal identification of union organizers were threatening measures. New registrations from a particular union could provide advance notice of an organizing campaign. The "Fats" Perrys and the

Worleys of the affected locale could start their
operations with accurate knowledge of their targets.

The Oil Workers Union had an organizing drive
mounted among the employees of Texas's wealth-
iest and most politically powerful industry. The Oil
Workers had invited R. J. Thomas, the president of
the already successful and powerful United Automobile Workers to come to Houston to address a
rally of the Humble Oil Company's Baytown plant.
Thomas was a good-natured, gravel-voiced, lifetime
auto worker and a devoted trade unionist. The
meeting and the Thomas speech were well advertised and the Texas attorney general surmised (with
good reason) that Thomas would ask the audience
to join the Oil Workers.

Thomas arrived at Houston, and on the day of
the meeting he was served with a restraining order
issued ex parte by a district judge in Houston on
application of the attorney general of Texas. The injunction forbade Thomas's soliciting memberships
in the Oil Workers while he was in Texas without
an organizer's card issued by the secretary of state.

Thomas had come a long way to make that
speech and make it he would. He had a prepared
manuscript. He read it to the audience of three
hundred people. Then he invited all three hundred
in the audience to join the Oil Workers. He told
them that if need be, he would sign them up himself. Then so as to have the matter exquisitely clear,
he addressed one particular oil worker, Patrick
O'Sullivan, by name and invited him to join the Oil

Workers. Immediately after the meeting Thomas was arrested and taken before a justice of the peace.

Dad had been called to Houston from Dallas in some haste and he was there to appear for Thomas and arrange bond. The next day Thomas went to Austin to appear before the district judge who had issued the temporary restraining order. Dad again appeared for him and argued the unconstitutionality of the act as a prior restraint on speech. The district judge rejected the constitutional argument and held Thomas in contempt of court for violating the ex-parte restraining order. He sentenced Thomas to $500 fine and five days in jail. Again Dad arranged bail pending appeal.

A petition for writ of *habeas corpus* was filed before the Supreme Court of Texas. Quickly and unanimously that court upheld the constitutionality of the statute. It also affirmed the contempt conviction and sentence.

An appeal was then taken to the Supreme Court of the United States. This Court did not find the case so simple. It received briefs and then heard oral argument twice on the First Amendment issue.

It decided the case in an opinion by Mr. Justice Rutledge that spoke for five of the justices, with four dissenting. Rutledge reasoned that the ban on solicitation was a restraint on speech itself. He said:

That there was restriction upon Thomas' right to speak and the rights of the workers to hear what he had to say, there can be no doubt. The threat of the restraining order, backed by the power of contempt, and of arrest for crime, hung over every word. A speaker in such circumstances could avoid the words "solicit," "invite," "join." It would be impossible to avoid the idea.

Thomas v. *Collins,* 323 U.S. 516, 534 (1945).

Mr. Justice Jackson planted his concurrence on broader grounds:

[I]t cannot be the duty, because it is not the right, of the state to protect the public against false doctrine. The very purpose of the First Amendment is to foreclose public authority from assuming a guardianship of the public mind through regulating the press, speech, and religion. In this field every person must be his own watchman for truth, because the forefathers did not trust any government to separate the true from the false for us.

Thomas v. *Collins, supra* at 545 (concurring opinion).

Thomas v. *Collins* (Collins was the county sheriff) became one of the leading cases on the interpretation of the First Amendment. Obviously, it declared the rights of trade unionists to solicit memberships without prior registration. But it also speaks to the right of free assembly. And indirectly it reinforced the rights of employers freely (absent threats or coercion) to express their own opinions about the labor unions that their employees might be thinking of joining. Somewhat incidentally, the Supreme Court decision also kept Thomas from spending five days in a Houston jail for contempt of court.

Dad's diffidence about discussing anything that represented personal accomplishment was extreme. I knew, of course, that he had defended Thomas. But I don't remember his ever discussing the case

with me, except to comment on how tired he was
when he got back from Houston. I knew that the
UAW's general counsel had argued the case in the
U.S. Supreme Court. I first read the Supreme Court
opinion thirty years later in the course of appellate
research on the First Amendment rights of employers under the National Labor Relations Act. It
was then I learned that Dad and Arthur Garfield
Hays had filed one of the briefs on the case in the
United States Supreme Court.

It was in the midst of World War II that I finally
became a lawyer. I had seen the practice of law too
close at hand and too early in my boyhood. As indicated earlier, after half a dozen years of working
in Dad's law office and watching the Texas law of
that period in operation, I rejected law as a career.
In 1938, I finally entered law school at night at the
Detroit College of Law. All those years Dad had
kept the idea of law school alive. He also had been
careful not to push it too hard.

My first contact with law school did not completely reassure me as to my new decision. For the
two preceding years I had been working for the
United Automobile Workers and had frequently
been in the news concerning its dramatic and
turbulent growth. Seated across from the dean
while he was studying my application, I saw that he
was disturbed.

"Now, Mr. Edwards," he said, "you work for the
United Automobile Workers?"

I answered that I did.

"Well," he said, "you know that a lawyer is an officer of the court. Do you think you can be sufficiently impartial to serve as an officer of the court?"

"Dean," I said, "your law school is full of employees of the automobile companies. Many of them are employed in the corporation personnel and labor-relation offices, and I bargain with some of them every week. I think I can certainly be as impartial as any of them."

"Well," he said, "I never thought of that. I never thought of that."

And the dean signed my admission card.

Lawyers who come to the bar by the night-school route have vivid memories of those years. Their wives do, too. The conflict between law school on one hand and job and family on the other is intense. From 1938 through most of 1943 I attended classes at DCL. Many of the professors I had were practicing lawyers or judges, and dedicated teachers into the bargain. I had no repetition of my reaction to Blackstone. I found the classes fascinating. But during those years also I saw the UAW organize two thirds of the automobile industry and helped in the process. Peg and I were married. I was appointed by a newly elected reform mayor of Detroit, Ed Jeffries, as director of the Detroit Housing Commission, Peggy gave birth to our first son, George, and twice I ran for and was elected to the Detroit common council. In addition, in the early war years I was deputy chief air-raid warden for Detroit, and for eight months I worked the afternoon

shift at the Timken Detroit Axle assembly line, trying to save money for Peg and our baby to live on
when I was called into service, as I knew I was soon
going to be.

The law is said to be a jealous mistress. With me
she had reason to take some offense. I took 8:00 A.M.
classes all those years and, into the bargain, classes
at night two or three evenings a week. I read law at
breakfast, at dinner—and in class. In spite of everything else, I rarely missed a class. When I was inducted in the army in 1943, I was just half a year
short of a law-school degree.

A few months later I was in basic training at the
Infantry Training Replacement Center at Camp
Wheeler, Georgia, when I got a letter from Dick
Sullivan, one of my law-school friends. He wrote
that the Michigan legislature had passed a law
enabling anyone who had been inducted into service when he was within half a year of graduation to
take the bar examination. If he passed, he would be
admitted to the bar and could begin to practice.
Sullivan wanted to know whether he should deter-
mine my eligibility, and if I proved to be eligible,
send me the necessary application.

The letter was so remote from rifle ranges, bayo-
net drills, and overseas shipments that it sounded
incredible. But in the meantime Peg had given
birth to our second son, James, and I had never
even seen him. No matter what happened at the bar
examination, I couldn't lose on a trip home. I wrote
Sullivan saying by all means proceed.

Three busy weeks later in the training cycle at

mail call there was my cherished daily letter from
Peg, plus a letter from Sullivan. It said that I was eligible. He sent me an application and the dates of
the three-day-long bar exams. All I had to do was
send in the application, secure an emergency leave
from the army, and be prepared to pass the exams.
The first seemed simple, the last two impossible.

My experience with army life was hardly exten-
sive at that point, but I already knew that in that organization, too, the pen was mightier than the word.
An oral request could be safely forgotten. A written
request must be answered. I wrote a careful application for emergency leave to take the bar exam, de-
tailing for nonlawyers what relationship the exam
had to a legal career. I was amazed at the first
sergeant's reaction. A few weeks earlier, at a period
of dead time in training, he had greeted my application for leave to go home for the birth of our second
child with a laugh and the navy adage, "The father
is essential to the laying of the keel, but not to the
launching of the ship." Now he read my application
with great care. "Bar exam," he said, "that's important." And he proceeded to tell me that he had taken
a year of law at his home in Springfield, Massachusetts. He added that he would see what he
could do. I settled down to wait, but without much
hope.

I did make one gesture in the direction of prepa-
ration. I wrote to Dad and asked him to get a copy of
Ballantine's bar review and to send it to me air
mail, special delivery. In about a week I received a

heavy package from Dallas plastered with stamps. By then I was even more pessimistic about the emergency leave. I threw the package, unwrapped, into the bottom of my foot locker, and there it lay until my last glimmer of hope expired when my battalion moved out on a Sunday for the two-week bivouac that ended the training cycle.

The 20-mile march out to the bivouac area was at night. We carried full field packs, rifles, bayonets, and helmets. We pitched tents after reaching the bivouac area. All the following day we were engaged in attack problems that required assaulting a big hill and then digging in on its military crests to resist counterattack. The two-man pup tents had seemed cold and uninviting the preceding night. By Monday night they looked like home. After chow the camp quieted down quickly.

I was sound asleep at 11:00 P.M. when the driver of the water truck woke me. He said, "Edwards, roll your pack, you're going into camp."

I said, "What for?"

The answer, "I don't know. The first sergeant said to bring you in."

Rolling my pack required stripping off half of the pup tent. My tent mate never woke up and I left him covered (somewhat) by the other shelter half to ward off some the cold rain that was falling.

At camp I was handed an emergency leave, travel orders, and vouchers. My leave started at 12:30 A.M. Tuesday—about forty-five minutes away. I was scheduled to catch a 2:00 A.M. train for De-

troit, arriving just barely in time to accomplish the
formalities of the bar interview and the three days
of written examinations. The return train schedule
would just get me back to Macon for next Monday's
6:00 A.M. report. The point was to keep me from
missing over five training days. A trainee who
missed six had to repeat the whole training cycle. In
this instance the army's interests and mine coin-
cided absolutely.

I headed for the barracks, got into class-A uniform, packed a bag, picked up the package from
Dad (still wrapped), and caught the last bus that
would get me to the train.

The train north was already overloaded when it
got to Macon. I found a spot near the baggage racks,
sat down on my suitcase, and unwrapped Ballantine. I never got a seat on that train all the way
north. I couldn't sleep; I read Ballantine all night
and a good portion of the next day. It was much too
late to learn law, but Ballantine did serve to remind
me of courses I had taken and forgotten. And it did
serve to drive Browning automatic rifles and chemi-
cal warfare and foxhole digging and rifle ranges out
of my mind.

I got to Detroit late Wednesday morning—just in
time to see Peg and Andy, to meet and hold our
brand-new, wide-eyed second son, Jim, to get a few
hours sleep, and to appear at the Michigan Bar Association interview before driving to Lansing for
the exams.

The exams were held in the Supreme Court
chambers in the Michigan state capitol. None of us

one hundred intense young men who gathered there
noticed its beauty. We were concerned only about
the exams. It didn't help my apprehensions to discover that everyone who was taking the exams had
spent the past three months on a professional bar-
review course.

The bar examiners started the proceedings by
distributing the list of subjects that were to be covered at each of the six morning or afternoon ses-
sions. There were several of the eighteen subjects
listed in which I had taken no law-school course.
This, however, was likely to be true about every
candidate, and I knew that the bar examiners grad-
ing made allowance for this contingency. As I
remember it the three courses I had not taken were
municipal corporations, federal taxation, and do-
mestic relations. I had already had a good deal of experience in Detroit city government with the first
and some in the course of living with the other
two—and then there was Ballantine. I read it at
noon recess, evenings, and early mornings.

Peggy had gone with me to Lansing. We stayed
in a house loaned to us by friends. Bar exams
notwithstanding, it was like a second honeymoon.
And like a honeymoon, it ended all too soon. I
finished the last exam Saturday afternoon just in
time to drive to Detroit, kiss Jim, Andy, and Peg
good-by, and catch the last train for Georgia which
would get me to camp in time to report at 6:00 A.M.
Monday. I may well be the only infantry trainee in
history to feel that the second week of bivouac was a
relief from pressure. Several months later in In-

fantry Officer Candidate School at Fort Benning,
Georgia, I got word that I had passed the bar exam. I
called Peggy, and then Dad.

Years later I went back to DCL, took three additional courses, and got my law degree. By then I had
gotten tired of having to tell this long a story in
order accurately to answer the question, "When did
you get your degree?"

All during World War II Dad was much ab-
sorbed in the problems of a young Negro named
L. C. Akins. One evening in 1941 Akins had been
about to board a streetcar on Commerce in downtown Dallas for his home in Oak Cliff. There were
a number of people seeking to board the car, and as
Akins mounted the step of the car, he either jostled
a young white woman or her husband thought Akins
did. The husband grabbed Akins from behind,
pulled him off the car to the street, and a fight followed instantly. The husband was a young white
police officer named Morris. He was off duty and in
street clothes, but he was carrying his pistol. Early
in the fight he drew the pistol, hit Akins on the head
with it, and then shot him through the body. In spite
of the wound, Akins grappled with Morris, and
Morris dropped the gun. Akins got hold of the gun,
fired one shot, and killed Morris. He then walked
two blocks to the police station, in the basement of
the city hall, and surrendered himself and the gun.

Self-defense is the cardinal defense to a murder
charge. Many men have successfully invoked it in
Texas murder cases where the deceased proved to

be completely unarmed—but the killer testified that he shot after seeing his opponent make a "hip-pocket move."

As Dad was many times later publicly to point out, no man in the history of Texas had ever been prosecuted for murder under facts such as those in the *Akins* case.

Nonetheless, prosecuted Akins was. He was indicted by an all-white grand jury, tried before an all-white jury, convicted, and sentenced to life imprisonment. On appeal, the Texas Court of Criminal Appeals reversed Akins's conviction because of a then recent United States Supreme Court case, *Hill v. State* (also from Dallas County), where there had been no Negroes on the grand jury that indicted Hill and it was shown that there never had been a Negro on a jury in Dallas County, although there were many Negroes qualified for jury duty in the county.

Akins was retried and this time was sentenced to death. This conviction was affirmed in the Texas courts. The United States Supreme Court granted certiorari and subsequently affirmed the conviction also, but by a divided vote. In the second indictment there had been one elderly Negro on the grand jury, but as the dissenters pointed out, the commissioners who put him there specifically testified that they only intended to pick one Negro.

Dad had not tried either case. Akins had been represented by W. J. Durham—an able and effective Negro trial lawyer. Dad, however, saw the case

as an outrageous example of white man's law and
sought in every way he could to call public attention to the injustice of the conviction and the sentence of death. Twice he addressed the Dallas Bar
Association, seeking to move it to seek commuta-
tion. With the execution set for October 6, 1945, he
wrote an article that was published in the September 15 issue of the *Nation*. In this forum he
pointed out:

> If the wounded survivor of the fight had been a white
> man, it is doubtful whether, anywhere in Texas, he
> would have even been indicted. It is certain that the
> white survivor of such a fight would not have been pro-
> secuted for murder with malice. And if he had been in-
> dicted and put on trial, it is absolutely certain that he
> would not have been convicted and given a death sen-
> tence. This being true, it is clear that Dallas and the state
> of Texas are about to put this man to death because he is
> black. And everybody in Dallas knows it. Twice I have
> made this statement publicly before the Dallas Bar Asso-
> ciation, and many times privately to other lawyers. Not
> one lawyer has denied the truth of the statement. One as-
> sistant district attorney refused to take part in the case
> because he said the Negro ought never to have been in-
> dicted. One appellate judge, off the bench, in conversa-
> tion, which he will deny, said, "Of course the nigger
> ought not to be executed, but there was not an error in
> the record."

He noted that the one Negro juror who had
been chosen on the second *Akins* grand jury was
eighty years old, barely literate, and that the commissioners deliberately limited Negroes on the
grand jury to a token of one. He concluded:

I repeat that I know, and the judge who tried the case knows, and everybody else in Dallas knows that no white man would have been convicted of murder in a case like this, that Akins was condemned to death because of the color of his skin. Every citizen who approves or condones this death sentence shares the guilt of this Negro's death.

Just a week before the October 6 execution date, the governor, Coke Stevenson, commuted Akins's sentence to life imprisonment.

Nine years later in 1954 Akins was released from prison on a conditional pardon.

Before going overseas I spent six months as a weapons instructor at the Infantry Training Replacement Center at Camp Maxey in Paris, Texas. Peg and our two sons lived during those months with Dad and Mother in Dallas. On some week ends I got there, too, and we filled the house up to a degree never rivaled by the USO visitors.

On many week ends I was required to stay in camp and Peggy made the 100-mile trip there by bus—not infrequently standing up all the way. On these visits invariably I found my little Yankee sputtering about a sign under which the bus traveled enroute. It was hung over the main street of Greenville, Texas, and read "The Blackest Land— the Whitest People." I tried to tell Peggy that expression of her sentiments about that sign on a Greyhound bus was not entirely safe, however constitutional it might be.

THE BLACKEST LAND—
THE WHITEST PEOPLE

IN THE SPRING, when farmers plow their fields in central Texas, the moist furrows shine like hard coal. They call their soil "the black waxy." Indeed, the land was black around Greenville and Dallas. "The Whitest People" part of the Greenville sign was, however, another matter. It served to assert either the nonexistence or the complete unimportance of the thousands of black Texans in the black-land area around Dallas.

In my youth the Negroes of Dallas were frequently treated as if they were invisible or couldn't hear what was being said about them in their presence. "Civil rights" were words that communists used. An "uppity nigger" walked in mortal peril. I am well aware that there is much to be added to such harsh strictures before the whole truth is told. As southerners have always insisted, there was more black-white daily contact than in the North. In addition, there was a good deal of familiarity, pleasantry, and friendliness. But the relationship was always a master-servant one. The master called the servants by their first names, but the

black servants always called the white masters
"Mister." And when there was economic generosity, it was the product of personal largess and
never the freely-arrived-at bargain between equals.
Always in the background there was the brutal presence of the Ku Klux Klan to enforce the unwritten
and the unbreakable code.

Dad did not succeed in changing that code very
much in his lifetime, but he surely tried. What he
had to say to Dallas in the days of my youth and
beyond sounds now like Justice John Marshall
Harlan, the elder, writing a lone dissent in *Plessy* v.
Ferguson in 1894. Several times Dad was invited to
address the Dallas Bar Association. It was always an
occasion.

One of his earlier speeches included the frank-
est kind of appraisal of the low public esteem in
which the legal profession was held. In the same
speech he paid his compliments to the federal judiciary as he knew it in a way calculated to make even
a later-day federal judge reflect:

Federal judges are given the unhesitating, unques-
tionable, almost unrestrained backing of the enormous
spy forces of the government, the federal marshals and
the army. Into court they come and men are made to rise
as if something holy were approaching and on the bench
they rule with a power mighty and well nigh irrespon-
sible.

They control the jury, they lecture and abuse citizens,
who theoretically have some rights, and they intimidate
the ordinary lawyer who does not represent large prop-

erty interests. Let the simplest and most kindly individual be placed in such an environment, and, unless he is a very rare, an extraordinary type of man, he steadily tends to become arrogant and dictatorial beyond expression.

On the last such occasion, Dad spoke to the Dallas bar in the fall of 1944. In one of his letters he referred to the origin of this speech. In the spring of that year the bar had heard an address by a lawyer that Dad described as a "tirade against the Negro race by a lawyer with a full set of Civil War prejudices." Dad had made a written protest about the speech and its contents. In response, the bar invited him to answer. The audience that gathered knew these circumstances in advance, and the adherents of the previous speaker were on hand.

Dad entitled his talk "Negro Progress and White Justice." He wasted no time in paying respects to the preceding speech:

You have heard recently an argument approving all our anti-Negro laws, and calling on you as patriots to resist any change in them at all; and particularly to resist ideas from the North—because, in substance, the Negro is really sub-human and we whites are the proud superior race, and we should maintain our position by all necessary means. The argument was full of scorn for the Federal government, the Supreme Court, and all ideas more recent than the Dred Scott decision of 1857.

Dad then turned to his main theme:

The important question is not our leniency, or our good nature, but whether we in the South have been, are, and intend to be just to the Negro and to give him his rights. The record is easily available.

It seems clearly to show that we have not been and are not just or fair to the Negro in law, in education, in economics, and in employment; and my observation is that Southern lawyers have been rather more remiss in all these respects than doctors, ministers, teachers, or laymen.

The essence of what passes for legal justice is a matter of power. Those who have the power, decide what they are going to call just and legal; and that it is. In the South, we, the whites, locally and just now, have all the power. We make the laws. We control the execution or ignoring of the laws. We appoint, select, and elect all officials, peace officers, and judges. We alone constitute the grand juries and all trial juries, civil and criminal.

Does any one think that a system of laws and justice so dominated exclusively by white men is equal justice to the Negro?

No one thinks it equal justice. We maintain this state of affairs because we now have the power and we regard ourselves as the superior race. The idea of human justice does not enter into the thoughts of those who advocate white supremacy, at all times, in all places, at all costs.

And the actual results of this white-domination attitude in the application and working of legal machinery are just what one naturally expects.

In spite of our accepting the 13th, 14th, and 15th Amendments and regaining our share in the National Government, Negroes have been deprived, effectively and substantially, of the right to vote until this very year. There are people planning even now shrewd devices to evade, avoid, and nullify the recent decision of the Supreme Court.

Negroes are deprived of jury service, and our scornful and continued evasions of the decisions of the Supreme Court are unworthy, it seems to me, of law-abiding citizens.

Negroes get the scantiest and most begrudged share in our educational system, which is supposed to be fair and impartial. At tremendous expense we maintain a great university and law school and medical school and dental school, and exclude Negroes from all of them and provide no equal facilities for Negroes otherwise. The only recent gains in education have been as a result of Supreme Court decisions and the rulings and influences of Federal administrative boards denounced so heatedly as "bureaus".

Negroes are nowhere given equal and impartial consideration save in the lowest ranks of unskilled employment. The only active force in labor for Negro justice is the CIO.

We have a whole code of special anti-Negro legislation aimed at putting Negroes at disadvantages whites would violently rebel at.

It seems to me that when white people, with all their power, refuse Negroes, solely because of their color, legal rights to vote, to jury service, to equal educational opportunities, to consideration for work on merit, they are seeking to gain an undeserved advantage in those respects which justice and law—even if it has to be Federal law—will eventually destroy.

Dad turned from this analysis of "white power" to recall some history.

This is my main proposition: Those who contend that we in the South alone can handle this problem and that we know how it should be handled and that all our special anti-Negro laws and customs are not only legal but just and good and should be defended, unchanged, at all costs, are trying to go back to the policy that failed before the Civil War.

We, in the South, were approaching a solution of the slavery issue before the Revolution. . . . Washington and Jefferson and Hamilton and Patrick Henry, all of whom regarded slavery as an evil they hoped would be abolished, never, I believe, would have followed the dif-

ferent path that led to the Dred Scott decision and the
Civil War.

We, in the South, made a terrible mistake when, in
the States' Rights Period, we assumed by ourselves to
settle the slavery issue by perpetuating and extending it
by violence. We were on the wrong side, and the event
showed we were on the weaker side.

Let us not repeat the pro-slavery error. For us, in the
South, now to contend that the problem of the Negro and
the white is purely local, is our own exclusive affair, is
just as wrong and unreal and certain of eventual defeat as
was the pro-slavery contention of Pre-Civil War times. In
fact it is the same contention.

Dad used the *Akins* case (detailed in the preceding chapter) as a dramatic example of unequal justice. He challenged anyone in the audience to say
that based on the facts in the *Akins* case any white
man would ever have been convicted of murder in
Texas.

He concluded on a hopeful note:

Yet even in this most difficult and emotion-charged
matter of Negro and white relations we have made
progress since 1865 and we have hope and prospects for
more progress if we do not turn back.

What progress we have made is due, it seems clear, to

1. Our acceptance of the amendments abolishing
slavery

2. The economic superiority of free over slave labor

3. Efforts in good faith on the part of many individ-
uals both in the South and in and from the North—to help
and co-operate with Negroes

4. Efforts of our colored fellow citizens to co-operate
with us in solving the problems brought by Emancipa-
tion

5. The deliberate effort of the Federal government
. . . to aid the progress of the Negro. . . .

All of the forces just named are forces for both Negro
Progress and for White Justice; and all, it seems to me,
ought to have the backing of all good men.

The applause from the audience was generous
but not unanimous. When Dad had finished this
speech, one of the lawyers in the audience arose
and made a motion to strike the speech from the
minutes of the Dallas Bar Association. Debate on
that motion raged for some time until it was finally
tabled.

Years later, Dad mentioned that the Dallas bar
never invited him to make another speech and
added, "I'm sorry about that. I had a number of
other things I wanted to tell them."

THE ROAD FROM
TEXARKANA

IN AUGUST, 1946, Peggy and I planned to visit Mother and Dad in Texas. I had not seen them since coming back from overseas. They were eager to see the boys, who were now five and two. I had come back to Detroit as president of the city council by dint of being elected first in the council race while I was in the Philippines and Peggy was doing the campaigning. With some part-time law practice the financial pressures of the service years were eased a little, and we had bought a new car. It was a small Nash.

Somewhat to our consternation, Clara Howard, a lady who worked for us, asked if she could join the expedition. She was a fine woman; we were fond of her and she of us. But there were problems. She was large. She was black. She was outspoken.

She had, for example, come back from a visit to Atlanta and told of a white man approaching her and saying, "Auntie, can you direct me to Davidson's department store?"

To this she had replied. "Nephew, I'm sorry, I just don't know where it is."

This was long before the days of Civil Rights

acts and Freedom Riders, and public accommodations were rigidly segregated. I wasn't at all concerned if Mrs. Howard was willing to play nurse-
maid. That role was understood and accepted.
But I was certain Clara didn't feel that way about
her relationship to our family, and I was not at all
sure that she would or could play the part. However, Clara had a granddaughter in Texas whom she
hadn't seen for years and she badly wanted to go.

I talked to her about the problems of the trip.
She said she understood them fully and that she was
sure there would be no trouble. And, indeed, there
wasn't—until we got to Texarkana. There, a road-
side restaurant looked like about the only plausible
place to eat. Most of the trip we had eaten dinners at
hotels in which Clara had been served at the table
with us, but here we planned to drive on to Dallas. I
inquired, and they said they would serve Clara only
at a take-out window. She said to go ahead and she
would go to the take-out window and eat in the car.

Nothing more was said and with everyone fed,
we started the last leg of our journey to Dallas. As
we left Texarkana, I was driving into the glare of the
setting sun. Peg started the process of getting the
two boys to sleep in the back. Clara settled down
beside me and promptly went sound asleep. There
was little traffic, and I settled down also for an
uneventful drive of nearly 200 miles.

Forty minutes outside of Texarkana, just as the
sun had finally sunk below the horizon, I saw a car
stopped on the right-hand shoulder of the road. Its

lights were on, its doors were open, and two men were standing beside it. The motor was running. All this I noticed casually, but as I passed the car, I came to abruptly. The two men wore white hoods over their heads and down to their waists.

I automatically increased speed and looked back in the rearview mirror. As I watched, both men jumped into the car, slammed the doors, and the car started up—fast. I felt instinctively that we were pursued. I pressed the gas pedal to the floor on the little Nash and reached around to snap the locks on the doors.

From the back seat came Peggy's voice, "What's wrong?"

I answered, "I don't know, but there's something wrong with that car behind."

By that time I had got the Nash over 80 and it was straining and swaying on the road. The rearview mirror told me that the car behind, a Buick, was easily overtaking us. I had pressed the Nash further than I felt was safe. The whole situation made no sense. Why should we be pursued? These two men were certainly in Ku Klux regalia, but maybe they were on some other business.

I eased the gas a bit and maintained position on the right-hand side of the road. The Buick was obviously going to catch up and I intended to let it pass. We were still going close to 80 when the Buick pulled even—and stayed there. I looked. The hoods over the heads of the two men were rubber and had eye and mouth holes. The man in the right-hand

seat had the window down and was shouting something that I couldn't hear. At the same time he
pointed to our car and made a gesture as if he was
striking with his fist.

I put on my brakes sharply and the Buick shot
ahead. It then slowed down and I sped up suddenly
with my horn going full blast and passed him—this
time taking over the middle of the road, with no in-
tention of yielding it.

We traveled in tandem for a few tense seconds.
Then the Buick slowed down, gave three derisive
blasts on its horn, swung around in a wide U-turn,
and headed back in the opposite direction.

Both boys and Clara had slept peacefully
through it all. As we drove on toward Dallas in the
deepening dusk, Peg and I talked in low voices
about what had happened and what, if anything, to
do. We guessed that Clara had got into some kind of
altercation at the take-out window and that someone had called ahead for this demonstration to scare
her.

I was not much tempted to stop in any of the few
small towns shown on the map between where we
were and Dallas in order to report the matter. The
largest of them was Greenville, with its "The
Blackest Land—the Whitest People" sign.[3] East
Texas officialdom in those days hardly needed notice that Klansmen were still on the road. For that

3. The sign was still in place in 1962 when our oldest son, George
Clifton Edwards III (then a student at SMU), went to the Greenville
High School to make a civil rights speech. In 1969 the sign was taken
down by Greenville's first woman mayor.

matter, what would we report? Two hooded men and a hostile gesture? There had been no weapon shown, no threat heard, and, thankfully, no injury. And to my astonishment and chagrin, I couldn't even report the license plate number of the Buick. I had never thought to look at it.

In the end, we decided not to tell anybody—Clara, the boys, or the family. It was a tell-one, tell-all situation, and it would surely have been a poor way to start a vacation. I didn't think we could revive the long-dormant Ku Klux Klan Act of 1871 in east Texas in 1946 on the facts we had available in this episode. But I wasn't a bit sure that Dad might not be inclined to give it a try.

There were two results from the experience. Peggy understood my concern during Camp Maxey days about her comments on the Greenville sign a little better. And when Clara rejoined us for the trip home, we headed due north to Oklahoma City, avoiding the Texarkana road altogether.

Mother came to Detroit on one of her rare visits in 1951 when I was sworn in as probate judge in charge of the juvenile court of Wayne County. She was then in her late seventies but very lively and interested in everything. Since on such occasions only nice things are said about the new judge, her delight lent warmth to the whole proceeding. I don't think anyone in the room needed to be told who she was, although I took great joy in introducing her.

Dad, of course, had met many of my friends on

his two prior visits. He knew, though I am sure
Mother did not, that a quarter of those in the
crowded courtroom were people who had been
with me in the two Detroit council-president cam-
paigns, but not in the unsuccessful 1949 race for
mayor. The mayor's race had really separated the
fair- from the foul-weather friends. Although the
friends in adversity got a warmer hand clasp, I was
glad to see them all; and doubly glad to have
Mother and Dad share in a wholly happy occasion.

It was the last time I was ever to talk with
Mother. Two days after Mother and Dad returned to
Dallas, they went out for dinner at a nearby restaurant in University Park. Mother suddenly slumped
in her chair and Dad had to catch her to keep from
falling to the floor. With some difficulty and with
some friendly help from a neighbor and my cousin
Walker, he managed to get her home. The doctor
diagnosed her problem as a stroke. When I got to
Dallas I found Dad more distraught than I had ever
seen him and I found Mother unable to recognize
me.

She lived for five more years. They were pain-
free. She was pleasant and cooperative. The stroke
had, however, completely wiped out her adult
memory, leaving only an occasional astonishingly
vivid recollection of her plantation childhood.
Someone had to be with her twenty-four hours a
day. There was a devoted lady who served as guard-
ian, companion, and nurse for eight hours a day, five
days a week. But for five years Dad performed those

functions the other hours of the days and nights and the two other days of the week. To know all that and to see them, as many times Peg and I did, sitting together in the porch swing in the evenings quietly holding hands was a love poem in itself.

On June 5, 1956, the supreme court chamber in the old capitol in Lansing, Michigan, was crowded. Chief Justice Dethmers was a no-nonsense presiding officer who had required a bit of persuasion to accept the appropriateness of Governor G. Mennen Williams (who had appointed me and who was a lawyer) introducing me to the court. The ceremony was brief, had gone smoothly, and was nearly over. The chief justice had indicated that at the end I would have an opportunity to introduce my family. I was awed by the event, and I had thought a good deal about what I would say when presenting Peggy, our sons George and Jim, and Dad. Mother's illness, of course, had not allowed her to come.

Suddenly I heard the chief justice introducing my father. He had done his homework: "Forty-six years of practice of law in Dallas—one of the distinguished lawyers in the field of civil liberties in the country—we would be glad to have a few words from you on this occasion." I had had no intimation of any such plan, and I was sure Dad hadn't. I held my breath. Without hesitation Dad arose and spoke from the position where he had been sitting in a voice loud enough to be heard throughout the chamber:

"Mr. Chief Justice, your honors, may it please

the court. Mrs. Edwards and I greatly appreciate the confidence and trust the great state of Michigan has placed in our son. In the words of Micah, we pray for him that he will do justly, love mercy, and walk humbly with the spirit of love which is our God."

He sat down. And everything that was said thereafter seemed a bit unnecessary.

Mother died that summer. Another stroke had left her unconscious. By the time I reached Dallas, she had gone. No matter how great the reason to anticipate her death, she had given us so much love that our grief was overwhelming. Dad mourned her like a lost bride.

TEXAS v. NAACP

DAD'S LAST IMPORTANT case started in the fall of 1956 when he was nearly seventy-eight years old. John Ben Shepperd, attorney general of Texas, decided to try to put the National Association for the Advancement of Colored People out of business in Texas. He filed a suit against the NAACP and its 113 Texas branches, alleging that they had violated Texas's corporation laws and the Texas law against barratry! On the basis of his bill of complaint and the affidavits he attached, and without hearing, the attorney general secured a sweeping temporary restraining order against the NAACP. Shepperd had chosen his judge carefully. District Judge Otis T. Dunagan was a boyhood friend of Shepperd's. He presided at Tyler in the heart of east Texas, which traditionally espoused the Deep South race practices of neighboring Louisiana. Judge Dunagan issued the restraining order ex parte on September 21, 1956. His public comment made the defendant's problems quite obvious: "We have got nothing against the niggers. We get along all right with them. But these nigger corporations have got to follow the law just as other folks do."

Judge Dunagan's restraining order "found" (from affidavits filed, of course, only by the attorney

general) that irreparable damage would befall the
state of Texas "before notice can be served upon the
defendants," unless the defendants were restrained
forthwith. And restrained the defendants were
"from further conducting their business within the
State of Texas," from organizing chapters, and from
soliciting money or fees "of any kind." A hearing
was set for September 28. Until then the NAACP
was out of business in Texas.

By 1956 the NAACP was no longer the small and
pitifully weak organization of preceding decades.
In the early fifties it had won a series of spectacular
victories in the Supreme Court of the United States,
culminating in 1954 in *Brown* v. *Board of Education of Topeka*—the fundamental school-desegrega-
tion case. It had formidable legal talent at its command. W. J. Durham, of Dallas, was a powerful trial
lawyer. Thurgood Marshall (now a justice of the
United States Supreme Court) was chief counsel for
the National Legal Defense Fund, the separate
legal affiliate of the NAACP.

Dad was aware that the NAACP was fully capable of handling its own problems—if legal knowledge and skill were all that was at issue. He, at
nearly seventy-eight, had no desire to participate in
the arduous trial work that was bound to come. But,
as he put it, he had "a concern" that there should be
"a showing made by some white southerner who
felt outraged by the unjust suit." Dad became secretary of the NAACP's defense. He prepared a trial
brief on the applicable law. He attended every
court session and took notes on each day's proceed-

ings. Since Marshall, Durham, Bunkley, and Tate, the NAACP lawyers who were actively trying the case, could not as Negroes find accommodations in Tyler, each day Dad drove with them from Dallas to Tyler before court, and after adjournment rode the 100 miles with them back to Dallas at night.

Justice Marshall told me that Judge Dunagan called him to the bench early in the trial to inquire, "What is that white lawyer doing with you?" Marshall told him that Dad had said he didn't want history to record that there was no white man in Texas who would stand up for the NAACP.

The weather was hot when the hearings started. Dad was amused by an undeclared rivalry between the eight or nine young attorneys general and the NAACP lawyers in showing up every day in different, freshly pressed suits of summer clothes.

Somewhat more important was the competition in the trial itself. As to this Dad commented:

> The court and the eight or nine assistants lost no time in recognizing that they had against them just as good brains and knowledge of the law and experience as were on the State's side. They quickly got used to the custom of addressing a Negro as *Mr.* Durham or *Mr.* Bunkley or *Mr.* Marshall or *Mr.* Tate. That seems a petty thing to mention, but it is part of the education the NAACP is doing in its efforts to uphold the personal dignity of the Negro. I have seen a Dallas judge very elaborately address a Negro lawyer as "Counseller" while he constantly used *Mr.* to the white lawyers.

The hearings on the temporary injunction continued for seventeen trial days. Much of it consisted of the state's introduction of masses of letters, records, and documents seized in investigative police raids on NAACP branches throughout Texas. All of this "evidence" was objected to as irrelevant and as not related to either the parent NAACP or to any branch other than the one from which it was seized. Justice Marshall remembers that there were over two hundred objections and that only one was sustained.

The trial came during the World Series. In younger years Judge Dunagan had been a baseball player, a pitcher. On a day when a crucial World Series game was scheduled, the parties agreed (for once) upon a motion for a recess to go over exhibits with a view toward stipulating admission of same and thus shortening the trial. The motion was granted, and while some unfortunate lawyers on each side worked on the stipulations, the balance of the lawyers and the judge listened to the World Series.

In spite of this interlude, the temporary-injunction hearing days were tension-filled. The courtroom was always crowded, and on the day the decision was to be announced, Dad noted that present in the courtroom were twelve state troopers, numerous plain-clothesmen, and a delegation from Houston carrying Confederate flags.

Judge Dunagan sustained the entire state's case, specifically finding as a fact that the NAACP was "a profit-making corporation," and that it dominated the 113 separate branches in Texas so as to make them agents. He then granted a temporary injunction with all the previously stipulated prohibitions. The NAACP was still out of business in Texas and would be until the case was tried on its merits.

The injunction is an instrument of awesome power, comparable in many respects to the edict of a king. Common law through the centuries has found no way to avoid giving some authority the right to use it. But it has hedged the injunction with a series of protective devices. In Texas, as in most states, a suit for injunction must go through three proceedings. The first is a restraining order, which can be issued without notice but must expire within ten days. After hearing, the restraining order may be turned into a temporary injunction. The temporary injunction, however, must still be followed by trial on the merits of the case. In this sense the NAACP had yet to have its day in court. In the temporary-injunction proceeding the advantage is usually with the moving party. John Ben Shepperd and his men were thoroughly prepared for the preliminary hearing and the NAACP had had just eight days to catch up. They would not be caught short again.

The case came up for trial in May, 1957. This time the scales of justice were much more evenly balanced. For one thing the defendants had had time to make arrangements for quarters in Tyler and the 200 miles of driving each day were eliminated. In addition, with time to prepare, the defendants were thoroughly ready to prove the nonprofit character of the NAACP's operation, both within Texas and nationally, and equally prepared to rebut the inferences of violations of Texas law that had impressed Judge Dunagan at the first hearing.

While the trial itself was lengthy and much of the evidence was documentary, the stakes were great and at times emotions were high. Attorney General Shepperd termed the NAACP leadership "cold-blooded" and "mercenary." He said:

> The NAACP purports to act in behalf of the people of their race, but all it has done, according to the evidence we have presented here, was to peddle false hopes.
>
> They have said pay us, and we will knock down segregation in the schools, in public pools, in recreation, housing, etc.

When W. J. Durham summed up for the defense, he castigated Shepperd and his men for their armed raids employing state airplanes and the Texas rangers to seize the records of over one hundred NAACP branches. He also attacked Shepperd for charging the NAACP with barratry for filing civil-rights cases when he, as attorney general, would not move to stop mob violence against a school child seeking her lawful right to go to school:

> I challenge the attorney general to say whether or not he would take a hand to help in the peaceful settlement of an incident in which a 17-year-old girl was confronted and threatened by a mob, menaced by persons who were acting in defiance of the judgment and decision of the highest tribunal in the land.
>
> The attorney general did not utter one word of objection when this child, seeking the education to which she is entitled, was met by an angry mob at Texarkana [Texas] Junior College.

In spite of the drama in the closing arguments, the final decree of the court had many aspects of a negotiated settlement. It is true that Attorney General Shepperd got his injunction, and the Texas press was able to praise him for it. In appearance the injunction was a longer and more formidable legal document than the two previous orders. In addition, it required the NAACP, as a foreign corporation, to pay franchise taxes to Texas in order to do business there, and it enjoined the organizations against violating a whole series of Texas laws. Thus, for example, the NAACP was prohibited from:

   (e) Hiring or paying any litigant to bring, maintain or prosecute a suit;
   (f) Engaging in political activities, contrary to the laws of the State of Texas; and
   (g) Engaging in lobbying activities contrary to the laws of the State of Texas; and . . .

Of course, the NAACP had always been subject to such prohibitions, and, significantly, this time there were no findings that it had ever violated any of them.

From the defendant's point of view, however, there was perhaps even more to rejoice about. There was a flat finding that the NAACP and the Legal Defense Fund were nonprofit organizations entitled to do business in Texas without a permit. Both organizations were enjoined from "doing other than educational and charitable activities within the State as are authorized by their respective charters." The temporary injunction was dis-

solved, and all other relief not specifically granted
was denied. The law suit had been long and costly.

The defendants might now be hailed into court
for any violation of Texas law in summary contempt
proceedings rather than be entitled to a full criminal trial. But the final fact was that the Texas
NAACP was back in business under a final decree
of entitlement issued by an east Texas district judge.

Talking of the case long afterward, Dad told me
that he considered Judge Dunagan's decision a
tremendous victory for the NAACP—particularly
when the east Texas locale and the massive effort by
the attorney general's office were taken into account.

NORTH—THEN SOUTH
TOWARD HOME

TWO MONTHS after decision of *Texas*
v. *NAACP*, Dad suffered a stroke. I was called from
a supreme court hearing in Lansing and took the
next plane for Dallas. I found him in bed, completely paralyzed on the left side. The paralysis affected his face and mouth and heavily slurred the
clear diction that I knew so well. The doctor's
prediction was optimistic as to recovery of at least
some of the damaged faculties, absent another
stroke.

After Mother's death Dad had refused to have
anyone with him in the house. My worst fear had
been a sudden illness, and it happened. The stroke
seized him in the early morning. He was alone.
Somehow he had enough warning to get to the
phone and to call my cousin Walker who lived
nearby. Walker came immediately, got him in bed,
called the doctor, and kept someone with him until
I got there.

Now I, who had received in earlier years so
much care and planning and tending, had the
chance to return some of these in kind. The doctor
had been negative on hospitalization, prescribing

bed rest, home care, and quiet. For the first two or three days and nights, until I was able to find adequate help, I tended to all his needs as you would those of a small child. I soon discovered that his mental faculties were as acute as ever, but the body would not respond. I discovered also that the decisive will had suffered damage. For the first time in his life he was willing—even eager—to have someone else make decisions for him.

The first night he was restless and I was up with him half a dozen times. Toward dawn he finally fell into a deep sleep and so did I, only to be awakened by the telephone. I reached it before the second ring and said, "Hello."

And a woman's voice said, "George Clifton Edwards?"

I said, "No, this is his son. It's six o'clock in the morning and Dad is asleep." I heard heavy breathing like an animal panting.

She said, "You tell that old son of a bitch I hope he dies and goes to Hell," and the phone clicked off.

I carried that message in my mind for forty-eight hours, until Carl Brannin showed me one of Dad's letters that had been published in the News a day or two before his stroke. The letter had defended the Warren Court and its decisions on school desegregation.

By the end of a week I had twenty-four-hour care organized and had Dad agreed upon coming north to Lansing with me when he could travel. I

didn't speak of it as a permanent move at first, although I hoped it would be. There was just too little
family left in Dallas. Dad's sister and all four of his
brothers had died before his stroke, as had most of
his old friends in Dallas. By the end of the week the
facial paralysis had lessened. Dad's left hand had
regained some finger movement and he could, with
effort, move his left leg slightly. I left for home with
some optimism.

Two weeks later I was back in Dallas to organize
the trip to Lansing. Now Dad could stand if I supported him. We took him by wheel chair and ambulance to the plane and by the same means to our
home in East Lansing. We moved the two boys
together into one room, and Peggy slowly nursed
Dad back to health. In six months he was up and
about and we moved him four doors away from our
house into an apartment with a housekeeper.

The Lansing years are hardly part of this story,
although they are very vivid in my mind. I like to
think of them as a quiet, sunny, and peaceful hiatus.
I am not sure, however, that Dad thought of them
just that way. Whenever anyone referred to his
"coming" to Michigan, he invariably responded,
"I didn't come, I was brought." To the end he
was very much a Texan. He missed its blue skies, its
hot sun, its people—and its problems.

He recovered completely from the paralysis
produced by the stroke. He had, however, aged
markedly with the illness. His mind was as clear as
ever, but his physical strength and his will had been

sapped. He resumed his reading, he picked up
some correspondence about his affairs in Dallas, he
began to write a little—mostly about the days of his
youth.

I saw him every morning on the way to work and
every evening before I returned home. He shortly
began to take a daily walk to the beautiful campus of
Michigan State University, spending an hour or so
at its library before he undertook the half-mile return. In the afternoons he came to our house for tea
with Peggy, or visited one of our East Lansing
friends. He particularly enjoyed visiting Anne
Green, one of our close friends who taught English
literature at East Lansing High School. Her husband says he learned to expect to come home in the
Michigan winter dusk to find Anne and Dad drink-
ing tea and talking about William Faulkner.

Dad enjoyed going to Sunday services at All
Saints Episcopal Church, which also served Michigan State University. The first such Sunday as
the church began to fill with townspeople and students and the organist began a familiar hymn, I
looked over and saw tears streaming down Dad's
face. At Sunday dinner he told Peg and me that it
was the first time he had ever seen black and white
people worshiping together in an Episcopal church.
He had thought he would never live to see it.

Dad's intellectual curiosity never diminished.
One evening I found him reading a thick volume
on electricity that he had brought home from the

library. My surprised "Dad, I didn't know you were interested in electricity!" was greeted by "Son, I'm a little bit interested in everything."

His concern about public affairs returned full force, and he took a vivid interest in what was going on in my work in the Michigan Supreme Court. I ran for re-election while he was in East Lansing. Peggy and I spent the evening with our campaign supporters in Detroit. I talked to Dad after the polls closed to tell him that there were probably not going to be any returns on my race until the next morning. When we did have solid good news, it was 2:00 A.M. and we were driving back to Lansing. It seemed too late to call. I gathered the next day that Dad had not slept all night.

We weathered two other serious illnesses together in Lansing. One was a strange internal bleeding close under the skin which turned big areas of his arms and legs black and blue, as if they had been badly bruised. Three weeks of hospital care and medication served to check the disease and he lived comfortably for another year.

January 30, 1961, I came by Dad's apartment to find him uncomfortable with some severe swelling in his left thigh. Our regular physician was out of the city and his associate diagnosed it as more internal bleeding. This time it was deep within the tissues of the leg. Out of his hearing, the doctor asked me Dad's age. I answered "Eighty-three," and he shook his head. He wasn't willing to risk surgery or even to try to hospitalize him, preferring to have his partner make the decisions the next morning.

I made plans to stay all night with Dad and as I tucked him in for the night, he asked me to bring him the book beside his chair that he had been reading when I arrived. He and I both knew that he was desperately ill, but he went to sleep that night reading Kirby Page's *Living Creatively*.

The next morning our doctor promptly ordered an ambulance. When it arrived one of the two attendants with the stretcher undertook to reassure the patient, "Now, don't you worry, we'll get you to the hospital and get you back here as good as new in no time at all."

Dad looked at him and responded dryly, "That would be quite an achievement."

Dad died in the hospital while a young nurse was struggling to find a vein that would receive a blood transfusion. I was with him at the moment of death.

We had a service for him at All Saints Episcopal Church in East Lansing, with friends of his and ours from all over Michigan. Then we took his body to Dallas, where his long and productive years had been spent. Mother, whose love for the Episcopal Church was both profound and untroubled, we had buried from the Church of the Incarnation. But for Dad we decided upon a funeral service at the Unitarian Church that Dad and Mother had attended every other Sunday. (Mother's version of their Sundays was "One Sunday we go to Church, and the next to the Unitarians.") The Negro friends of our family had not attended the service for Mother at the Church of the Incarnation. I didn't know whether they would have been refused admittance if Dad's funeral was held there—but I was in no mood to find out. At the Unitarian Church, presided over by Dr. Raible, I was sure that all of God's children were truly welcome.

I made up the funeral announcement, including the list of pallbearers. The males of our family in Dallas had been decimated by death (natural and World War II) and reduced by departures like mine. There were only two Edwards men left—William and Walker Edwards, first cousins toward whom I felt great affection. We had grown up in the same neighborhood in Oak Lawn. We had never been particularly close as boys, since they were a couple of important years older than I. But after I left Dallas, they had lived and worked in close proximity to Dad. He had taken care of their legal affairs, and they had frequently helped him in much the sort of way I would have wanted to had I been in Dallas. He had been very fond of them and they of him. They were first on the list of pallbearers. It also included Carl Brannin, Dad's lifetime friend and associate in many causes, and two Negro friends, W. J. Durham, the trial lawyer in the *Texas* v. *NAACP* case, and another Dallas Negro leader and friend, A. Maceo Smith.

The day before the funeral I got a call from Bill Edwards. He said, "George, Walker and I can't be pallbearers tomorrow."

I said, "Bill, that's terrible news. I called you. We're depending on you."

"Yeah," he said, "but you didn't tell me you were going to have nigger pallbearers too."

I didn't say anything for a long moment, but finally managed, "I'm awfully sorry, Bill. I'm sorry for Dad and I'm sorry for you."

The day after the funeral William Edwards had a heart attack. There were, of course, other reasons for the heart attack, and I profoundly hope the pallbearer matter had nothing to do with it. I had not thought of the possibility of that sort of reaction to the eternal problem. If I had, I would certainly have given warning in advance.

Perhaps it is appropriate that the race problem followed Dad literally to his grave. He had lived with it all his life.

The funeral was an ingathering of friends. Dad had outlived most of his family and many of his compatriots. But the church was full of people whom in one way or another he had served or inspired. There were former clients and former pupils and fellow lawyers and judges, and many of the younger generation of Dallas to whom Dad had been a symbol of the social and legal pioneer. At least a third of those present were Negroes or Mexican Americans. Peg and Nicky and I felt that we were the objects of much transferred love.

A PROPHET IS NOT
WITHOUT HONOR

THIS COLLOQUY took place on the
first day of the Senate hearing on my confirmation as
a federal appellate judge:

Senator Ervin. Your father was a member of the Socialist Party, was he not, for a time at least?

Judge Edwards. I would say, Senator, that he probably was the best known Socialist in the State of Texas for
most of his life.

I might add, this was not a post for which there was
keen competition.

Most of his life in Dallas my father lived with
public and newspaper scorn for his beliefs and for
his social and political activities. As far as Dallas
was concerned, he was a good fifty years ahead of
his time. There were, however, friends and admirers even in his own country. On the fiftieth anni-
versary of his beginning the practice of law in
Dallas, a group of his friends gave a reception for
both Mother and Dad and presented Dad with a resolution honoring his fifty years of public service in
Dallas. The events referred to were a summary of
his life. I was asked to and did contribute the last
two paragraphs of the resolution:

WE SALUTE HIM:

As the founder and teacher of the first free night school in Dallas;

As a "poor man's advocate" defending those who came to him needing aid regardless of race, creed, color or ability to pay;

As a one-man committee for civil liberties speaking out for often unpopular causes where they concerned the rights and welfare of wage earners and minorities;

As an outspoken champion of equal rights for Negroes and an opponent of all types of discrimination.

All his life he has pursued virtue both personal and political, with the fierceness of the early Prophets and with about the same inclination toward compromise.

All his life he has been a pioneer on the social frontiers of our times. Much of what he has advocated has come into being.

At his death even the *Dallas Morning News* saw more good in his career than it had observed in his lifetime:

George Clifton Edwards—teacher, lawyer, political philosopher—is dead at 83. Socialist candidate for governor in 1906, later a dedicated New Deal liberal, Mr. Edwards spent most of his life in Dallas, later moved to Michigan to be with his son.

Mr. Edwards disagreed with about 95 per cent of The News' political editorials and didn't fail to say so in letters for publication on this page.

But The News always was glad to hear from him. He was honest in his belief, dedicated in his liberal principles, articulate and fair in his expression. You must admire any man like that.

If my father had heroes in his lifetime—and there may be doubt that that's the right word—aside from Christ and Tolstoi, they were Gene Debs and Norman Thomas.

In time he came to revere the Roosevelts, Franklin and Eleanor, not for what they said, but for what he had seen them do—for this country and for the world.

All his life he was fond of quoting Gene Debs's famous words at the Pullman-strike trial:

> Years ago I recognized my kinship with all living beings and made up my mind that I was not one bit better than the meanest of earth. I said then, I say now, that while there is a lower class I am in it, while there is a criminal element, I am of it, while there is a soul in prison I am not free.

Debs, however, died in 1926. He was a figure of heroic proportions in American social history. But Thomas was one of Dad's contemporaries and undoubtedly came closer than anyone to representing on the national scene my father's social and political concerns. Thomas came to his socialist convictions through the ministry. Throughout his life his message was consistently more concerned with morality than what is normally termed politics. His power with people, particularly with the young, lay in the depth and earnestness of his convictions. In an accurate employment of the term, Thomas was a Christian socialist.

Although he did not talk much about religion, my father's political beliefs were similarly rooted in religious beliefs.

Long after his death I came upon this statement

of Dad's faith, written in his unmistakable small
script:

God is not the clear, definite idea and person of the
catechism—to us bewildered and strained beings.

When I try to be plain and frank with myself, as I
might be if I were trying to express my ideas to friendly
and sympathetic persons, I find words about like these:

I believe in goodness, that it exists now, and has
always existed since men attained consciousness, in
some or all men in varying degrees.

I believe that the source of goodness is only partly in
our individual selves.

I believe that goodness, courage, tenderness, striving
for the right, justice, conscious good will and love
toward all men are realities; and that these realities
should be the guides by which we try to lead the good
life.

The source of goodness in ourselves and the power
that has been realized in goodness in times past is what I
think of as God—spiritual, infinite, incomprehensible,
and to whom I try to pray, not as asking and expecting
gifts or things, but as an effort to clarify my mind and to
ascertain His will and to cooperate.

Dad once wrote his political beliefs for his Harvard class book:

"The one distinctive feature of my life has been my
belief in and work for Socialism," Edwards writes for this
Report. "Socialism has been my inspiration, my philosophy, and my guide for action. For me it explains how society has become what it is and what its tendencies are
for the future. It shows what economic and political action one should support. It is the means by which human
brotherhood, the highest development of the individual,
and social justice may be attained.

"After the first World War, we saw our criticisms of
the capitalist system documented under Harding, Coo-

lidge, and Hoover. In 1932 Roosevelt adopted many of our criticisms and some of our immediate but not radical platform demands. He also took most of our members and the Texas Socialist party faded out. Since that time, for the past ten years, I have voted for the Democratic party and have worked for the unions, the Negroes, the Mexicans, the victims of loan sharks, and for working people generally as best I could in the party and in my law practice. I have always been on the other side from the rich and the exploiters, in theory and in fact.

"Holding such convictions, as I look back over the years since '99, I find little of which to be personally proud and much about which to be humble and chagrined. If hell is paved with good intentions, I have furnished quite a block there. I have wanted to help the poor and needy but my efforts in Dallas, Texas, against the forces producing poverty, injustice, and violence have seemed almost like whistling against the north wind. . . .

"Yet I am not pessimistic about the future if only the world does not commit suicide by atomic war. The European Recovery Program seems an unparalleled and civilized undertaking—an effort to save human lives and values that, as far as the American people are concerned, is free from any imperialistic design. The United Nations seems at times a very sickly plant and more like the Continental Congress than government under our present constitution, but the Continental Congress and our early constitutional government were sickly plants at first and for years.

"The current civil rights program and discussion are proof that democracy is struggling in America to end the disgrace of racial intolerance. Further, the coming of electricity to farms and ranches and villages that private companies failed to serve, the growing appreciation of regional planning like the T.V.A., the recognition of social responsibility for the aged and the unemployed, the certainty that we shall settle the housing problem some day in spite of the real estate capitalists, the advance of the Negro towards political rights—all are achievements that in '99 would have seemed fantastic hopes.

"For fifty years I have been dissatisfied with capitalism, and for almost as long disgusted with the way many of our politicians have indulged in ignoble racial injustices and at the same time have played the stooge to exploiting Northern capital. But as I end these lines which the few readers our Class will provide must think strange from a man who regards himself as fortunate, I ought to add my gratitude for much in my long life—from the devotion of my post-Civil War parents whose hardships in the broken South of the 1870's few Harvard men can have any notion of, down to a most favored old age. A family appreciative beyond my deserts, interesting work, good health, good eyes, good books, Texas sunlight, and hope for a finally just and democratic society—who could reasonably ask for more?"

A number of times as a boy I heard my father threaten, jokingly, to haunt anyone who wrote about him after he died without saying that the most important thing about him was that he was a socialist. The threat never seemed to be aimed at me—but I don't want to take a chance. So I have let him tell you that himself, just as he did to his Harvard class of 1899.

It seems to me, however, that the most important function of language is to clarify, and the term *socialist* has been so much abused that I doubt it clarifies much of anything in modern-day America. To some, the word *socialist* means an advocate of violent revolution and dictatorship—doctrines that were anathemas to my father. To others who might know the language better than that, the word still conveys a concept of a Utopian dreamer who deliberately chooses to live with ideals as opposed to reality. I don't think that concept fits the picture either.

Uncompromising as Dad was in his beliefs, he was never a political dilettante. He lived with and in the issues of his times and tried to do something about them.

Dad had no use for pseudointellectuals who elevated economic or political propositions into religious dogmas. And he instinctively rejected those theoreticians in the Socialist party and elsewhere whose eyes were turned backward to the causes and issues of the countries in Europe from which they had long since departed or fled.

He was a midwestern American who loved the land and the sun and the people of Texas. In many ways he was close kin to midwestern populism. He was against big finance, big business, corrupt government, and callous bureaucracy. He was for little people, the crippled, the ill, the poor. He was for labor, for Negroes, for progress. He admired doers. He had fought for many humanitarian programs all of his life. By the late thirties many of these identical plans had been brought into existence by the leadership of Franklin Delano Roosevelt and the dynamics of his New Deal. Dad's conviction that Hitler had to be stopped at all costs had already made him reject absolutely the World War II neutrality position of the Socialist party. When young

New Dealers began to organize liberal forces in the Texas Democratic party, Dad was quick to join them.

Whatever was going on in Dallas, in Texas, the United States, or the world, Dad was interested. He was likely to have an opinion on it, and if he did, he felt inclined—perhaps duty-bound—to share it with those most concerned. These latter did not always appreciate his generosity. My point is simply that no one who ran a one-man law office for the poor and black and downtrodden in the early 1900s on Main Street in Dallas, Texas, could properly be thought of as a dreamer. His office in those days had too many of the aspects of a battlefield casualty station.

In the first decade of this century Dad outlined in the *Laborer* the issues to which he would devote his life. They matched the concerns of the forces for social progress in American through the years. In the order they appeared in the *Laborer*'s pages they were:

> Freedom of speech
> Compulsory education
> Abolition of child labor
> The graduated income tax
> Eight-hour work day
> The right to organize
> Public housing for low-income families
> Mine-safety legislation
> Women's suffrage
> Workmen's compensation insurance
> Old-age insurance
> Equal rights for Negroes
> Abolition of capital punishment

Every one of these issues was highly controversial in its time. My father was bitterly attacked, sometimes physically endangered, for advocating them. Dad seemed to consider his lifetime of social and legal pioneering to have been something less than a success. But every one of these changes has now become an accepted part of American life and American law.

In my father's lifetime the United States of America changed profoundly from a nation that boasted that as the exponent of uncontrolled capitalism it had no social conscience to a nation that was eager to assert that it did. How much of this change was due to pioneers like him probably no one can ever assess.

Dad was a unique mortal! Yet in many respects his life typified the fierce independence, the integrity, and the social vision of those who, through two centuries, have created the American Dream.